FIVE STEPS TO CONQUER

'DEATH BY POWERPOINT'

FIVE STEPS TO CONQUER

'DEATH BY POWERPOINT'

CHANGING THE WORLD
ONE CONVERSATION
AT A TIME

Eric Bergman

Petticoat Creek Press Inc.

Author: Eric Bergman
Executive Editor: Roberta Resnick
Design: Deana De Ciccio
Publicity: Advantis Communications Inc.
Social Media Coordinator: Sacha Vaz
Website Coordinator: Maia Doytcheva
Media Kit Coordinator: Alexandra Muszynski-Kwan
Media Relations Coordinator: Michael Giardino
Author Photo: Alan McKenzie
PowerPoint® and Word® are trademarks of Microsoft Corp.
Keynote® and Pages® are trademarks of Apple Inc.
Prezi® is a trademark of Prezi, Inc.

ISBN-13: 978-1469926377

Table of Contents

Author's Preface: Five Simple Steps

1. Put the audience first
2. Structure the conversation
3. Minimize visual aids
4. Convey your message and personality
5. Answer questions throughout

This book is designed for two groups. The first is presenters. It doesn't matter whether you read a single additional word in this book, if you embrace these five steps and actively incorporate them into your presentations, your communication effectiveness will improve. Please allow these five steps to help you be even more successful in the future.

The second group is audiences; everyone who has had to endure mind-numbing, slide-driven presentations delivered by others. I encourage you to insist that these five steps be incorporated into every presentation delivered to you—whether in the boardroom, meeting room, training room, classroom, conference hall, or other venue.

If we can complete the two parts of the whole—improving presentations on one hand while setting a higher standard on the other— we really will improve the world, one conversation at a time.

—*Eric Bergman*

Foreword

Presentations are stereotyped. A speaker stands in front of an audience, uses PowerPoint to guide a talk, and says very little that departs from the PowerPoint presentation. Frequently, the speaker provides a handout or electronic version of the PowerPoint as a record of the talk. Depending on the nature of the talk (lecture to students; conference presentation; talk to a business group), a few minutes may be left at the end for questions. Readers will recognize this format as an almost universal one.

Stereotyped human behavior can be useful because it allows us to determine how to behave without having to continually invent new behaviors. Of course, stereotyped behavior is only useful if it is functional. If it is dysfunctional, it should be changed.

Eric Bergman believes that the procedures we habitually use during presentations are dysfunctional and in dire need of a change. As someone who has yet to listen to (or read!) a stimulating PowerPoint presentation, I find it very easy to agree that change is needed. However, the question becomes: How should we change?

This book provides us with an essential guide. While guides to any number of human activities are a dime-a-dozen, this one is different. Yes, readers may feel that the suggestions articulated here are a radical departure from what currently occurs, but how do we know it is any better than the stereotype? Bergman is clearly enthusiastic, but the changes he advocates are very large. Why should we make such large changes because he personally feels it would be an improvement?

In fact, the recommendations in this book reflect much more than the personal views of one author, albeit a very knowledgeable one. The various recommendations Bergman makes are based on strong research evidence he has brilliantly applied to the art of presenting information to a live audience.

This book is directed at practitioners rather than researchers. Therefore, it is inappropriate to discuss the research base of the book in detail; those details can be found elsewhere. For readers interested in the research base, and for those already familiar with cognitive load theory and its effects, here are some very brief pointers. The recommendation to avoid PowerPoint as a visual version of a talk is based on the redundancy effect, as is the recommendation that answers to questions should be brief and to the point. The recommendation to allow questions during a talk rather than at the end is based on the temporal split-attention effect. The suggestion that talks should include sufficient pauses to allow an audience to think flows from cognitive load theory and its emphasis on a limited working memory, based on empirical findings associated with massed versus spaced practice.

Today we use technology such as PowerPoint because we can, not because it results in improvements. I feel the evidence is overwhelming that the way in which we currently organize presentations is ineffective and inappropriate.

The strong research base that underpins this book provides reassurance that the recommended techniques have been tested and actually do work in a variety of contexts. Readers should try these recommendations for themselves.

This well-written, fascinating book provides us with effective presentation techniques, rather than the ineffective ones that have arisen without sufficient thought or consideration of their consequences. Eric Bergman's techniques are a window to the future of this important human activity.

—*John Sweller, Ph.D.*
Professor Emeritus
University of New South Wales
Sydney, Australia

Picture the poor lemming.
Its peers are rushing by, so it stops one and asks:
"Where are you going?"
"To the cliff."
"What's a cliff?"
"It's where you jump."
"What happens when you jump?"
"I don't know. Listen, I gotta go. You coming?"
"Not this time. You jump and then come get me.
I'll go with you the second time around."

Introduction:
The Pied Piper of PowerPoint

When it comes to informing, teaching, and persuading others through presentations, it's simply astounding that well-educated, highly qualified, and successful people—who would challenge any assumptions related to their area of expertise—will quietly take for granted the science and theory of effective communication. What's even more astonishing is that they do so on the basis of one simple statement: "That's the way it's done."

Physicians who wouldn't prescribe anything stronger than ibuprofen without clinical trials will deliver 100+ slides during a continuing medical education (CME) workshop to their peers. When you ask those doctors why so many or why slides at all, they'll tell you "that's the way it's done."

Executives who wouldn't make a single decision without reviewing net present value calculations against a range of alternatives will sit quietly while their senses are numbed during briefings. Nobody questions the value of projected slides and printed presentation decks, how they're presented, or whether separating orality (spoken language) and literacy (written language) might improve productivity and decision making. After all, "that's the way it's done."

On the basis of one simple statement: "That's the way it's done."

Investment managers who wouldn't invest a single penny of client money without conducting thorough research will happily bring a thick presentation deck to annual client updates. They never question whether simple alternatives would increase client understanding about how money is invested, or how the person making investment decisions is adding value. They never question whether clients asking dozens of questions are more important than any slide, or whether bringing slides in the first place interferes with the question-and-answer process. "That's the way it's done," they'll tell you.

Boards of directors will receive information about complex hedging strategies through projected slides, printed presentation decks, and oral presentations—all at the same time! Would research on informed consent around the principle of "less is more" potentially improve decision making? Probably. Would a format that allows more questions to be asked by directors per unit of time enhance understanding and ultimately improve decisions? Absolutely. But these directors sit quietly through the presentation before asking one or two questions at the end, because "that's the way it's done." Then they'll make their decision.

Professors in communication management at master's degree programs will project slide after slide or go through one presentation deck after another in the classroom. Research into best practices of adult education indicates that greater equality between facilitator and students (especially those with extensive industry experience like master's degree students) enhances the learning experience for everyone involved, including the professor. And while at least one credible educator has asserted that the world's most popular slideware program creates a power relationship between sender and receiver that's anything but equal, they continue to use slides as the basis for teaching, because "that's the way it's done."

If master's level students in communication management are wading their way through projected and printed slides, imagine what's taking place in undergraduate classrooms, not to mention conferences, workshops, plenaries, updates, annual meetings, management meetings, service meetings, sales meetings, staff meetings, foundation presentations, sales calls, training programs, seminars, teleconferences, short list presentations, investment reviews, pension board meetings, audit committee meetings, and marketing meetings the world over, every single day.

"That's the way it's done" has led us to where we are today. We now have a new phrase to express the phenomenon: "Death by PowerPoint."

And it's killing us.

PowerPoint: Not the Problem

Let's be clear here. PowerPoint is not the problem. PowerPoint is not flawed. The program simply has become a victim of its own success. PowerPoint has the task of enabling words, graphs, and images to be projected onto a screen or printed horizontally. The software program was originally designed to emulate 35-mm slides, at a time when slides cost fifty to one hundred dollars each to produce. PowerPoint completes its assigned tasks as well or better than anything else on the market. You simply click to add text, and start typing.

In the old days, we all knew
what it was like to overdose on overheads.

As we'll explore, therein lays the problem. Once you start adding text, when do you stop? You end up with a document that makes perfect sense to you, but isn't as well understood as you would have hoped. However, imagine for a moment that you had to take one hundred dollars out of your budget for every slide you used. Every slide would suddenly have value and this book would never have been written.

Microsoft has created a program that has taken the world by storm. PowerPoint is the market leader and 'Death by PowerPoint' is a catchy phrase. If another program was the market leader, the expression could very well be "Killed by Keynote" or "Pummeled by Prezi." Trust me, in the old days, we all knew what it was like to *overdose on overheads.*

No; PowerPoint is not the problem. The problem lies with assumptions underlying its use. Those assumptions are moving us further and further away from conversational exchanges when people get together. Correcting 'Death by PowerPoint' has little to do with good design, using images, incorporating video, or posing questions on your slides, which is how most pundits attack the problem. It lies with the underlying assumption that slides are actually necessary or desirable in the first place. The depth to which this fundamental assumption is ingrained in our social psyche is a testament to the effectiveness of the marketing department at Microsoft, and at 3M before that. They played the tune. We followed along.

Deeply Ingrained Assumption

How deeply ingrained is the underlying assumption that slides are essential? I was once asked by a pharmaceutical company to deliver a one-and-one-half hour presentation to a group of urologists who had gathered to put the finishing touches on a continuing medical education (CME) program. My role was to talk about how they could communicate their knowledge effectively when they later fanned out to conduct workshops across the country.

He didn't use slides.

The meeting took place at a resort that was absolutely beautiful, but in a remote location. I arrived the night before and had a quiet evening. I awoke early and decided to watch the presentations that preceded my talk.

From 8:30 to 9:15 a.m. one of the urologists stood at the front of the room and took thirty or so of his peers through the information they would later be asked to present. To my very pleasant surprise, he was a brilliant communicator. He didn't use slides. He showed two short videos. Most importantly, he created a conversation with thirty of his closest colleagues. In forty-five minutes, he provided incredible insight and answered close to a hundred questions. It was a case study in communication effectiveness. Everyone was engaged.

During a short break after his talk, I circulated through the room and noticed that people were talking in small groups. There was a buzz in the room. Everyone was commenting on how much they learned, and how the session was one of the best (if not the best) they had ever attended. After the break, they broke into groups to put the finishing touches on their PowerPoint slides.

There was a buzz in the room.

This exercise took longer than anticipated. No surprise there. When they reconvened at 11:40 a.m., I had twenty minutes before we had to break for lunch. I could have given a short version of my presentation, but I didn't.

These are highly educated individuals, I thought to myself, so I'm going to challenge them a bit. I focused their attention on the presentation we had witnessed earlier. They agreed it was brilliant. Everyone learned a lot. I then asked how many slides their colleague used. This caught them by surprise. It took a couple of minutes before they realized he hadn't used any, and, since he was still in the room, he verified the claim.

Then I asked if they were going to use the PowerPoint slides they spent the past two-and-a-half hours working on when they delivered their own CME sessions. They said yes. I asked: "Why?" At first there was silence. Then they pushed back.

That's the way it's done, and that's the way it's always been done.

To say that this evolved into a spirited conversation would be an understatement. Anyone watching would have thought I had refuted the holy grail of urology without a single shred of evidence. "That's the way CME programs are delivered," one physician commented. Another told me that CME programs had been delivered that way since speakers actually carried carousels of 35-mm slides from presentation to presentation. That's the way it's done, and that's the way it's always been done.

Perhaps, I said. But is that the best way? Wouldn't it be better to recreate what we all witnessed earlier?

My parting thought was that I hoped they would bring a similar analysis to the communication process that they bring to their profession. There's no doubt that communication is an art. But make no mistake, there's a growing body of social science research around communication. This research needs to be understood and properly applied.

However, the bottom line on communication effectiveness is simple. What someone says to an audience is relatively unimportant. The only thing that counts is how the audience applies the information or takes action on it. As a parting thought to this group of urologists, I expressed my hope that their next CME planning process would spend more time discussing how the earlier presentation could be emulated, if not recreated across the country, and less time putting the finishing touches on their slides.

Two Simple Statements

During a period of more than ten years, I asked more than twenty thousand people at workshops, seminars, and presentations to respond to each of the following statements in turn:

- Raise your hand if most of the business presentations you've attended in the past few years have made extensive use of visual aids.

- Raise your hand again if you can say that 51 percent or more of the presentations you attended in that period were a good use of your time.

Virtually every hand has gone up to the first statement. I think the only people who didn't put up their hands were too tired, too skeptical, too cynical, or too independent. Everyone knows that modern presentations are accompanied by slides—either projected, printed, or both. We've been visual-ed to death ever since acetates first met laser printers, and overhead projectors began popping up in meeting rooms, training rooms, and boardrooms throughout the world.

Response to the second statement has been interesting. At the workshops, presentations, and seminars I've facilitated, about 6 to 8 percent of people put up their hands. There is no question that less than 10 percent of more than twenty thousand people asked say that more than half of the presentations they had attended were a good use of their time. Regardless of how you examine them, these are poor results.

The vast majority of presentations
are ultimately wasting people's time.

What do these results tell us? The vast majority of people use visual aids when attempting to communicate with their fellow human beings. We know that. But the vast majority of the presentations delivered around the world on a daily basis are ultimately wasting people's time. The promise of technology was to improve productivity, not kill it. And that much wasted time is anything but an improvement.

However, isn't this entire process supposed to be about the audience? If it is, then what we're doing isn't working very well. We now have a vicious cycle. Someone will sit through a PowerPoint presentation and their eyes will glaze over. When it's their turn to develop a presentation, they'll turn on their computer, open a slideware program and click, type, and pray.

But therein lays the problem. Most people rely on PowerPoint (or Keynote or Prezi or SlideRocket or others) for most of their content development. I have come to the conclusion over the past twenty years that there's a direct correlation between the likelihood of boring others and the percentage of content development time spent sitting at a slideware program.

At my presentations and workshops, I now often ask people to respond to three statements in sequence. I ask them to raise their hands if they:

- Use PowerPoint or Keynote to develop content.

- Have experienced 'Death by PowerPoint' as a member of an audience.

- Have inflicted 'Death by PowerPoint' on others.

Almost every hand is raised to the first question; most people use some form of slideware program to prepare their presentations. The vast majority of hands go up to the second question; most people have experienced some form of 'Death by PowerPoint' as a member of an audience. Interestingly, virtually no one raises a hand to the third question. Obviously, very few people who inflict 'Death by PowerPoint' on others have attended one of my workshops.

Audiences are forced to work
very hard to extract value.

We're now at the point where audiences are forced to work very hard to extract value from any presentation. How many times have we heard someone say they always try to get at least one thing out of a presentation, a workshop, or a conference? Why can't they just sit back, listen, ask questions, and be prepared to comfortably apply a range of ideas when they walk out of the room?

Yes, it's intimidating to conduct a presentation. Everyone is looking at you. At times like this, you feel like you've morphed into another being. Adrenaline is not your friend. For some, it's akin to an out-of-body experience. They enter a surreal state.

All this is true, especially if you view the communication process as a presentation instead of a conversation. But it's a lot less intimidating to conduct a conversation, whether with two people or two hundred. We need to find ways to create productive conversations that are two-way, receiver-driven, and adhere to the fundamental principle of "less is more." Evolution has brought us tens of thousands of years of improving conversations, both one-on-one and with groups. It's time we put those skills to use.

Conversations Have Value

There is no doubt that conversations have value. For example, let's suppose you have a 1:00 p.m. meeting with a colleague, client, or boss. You arrive at that person's office, and you both realize that you haven't eaten. You decide to make it a working lunch.

There is one item on the agenda, the reason for scheduling the meeting in the first place. You're ready to present a new idea to the other person, with the goal of obtaining buy-in or approval. You finish lunch, and then devote ten minutes to your agenda item.

Would you be able to talk intelligently to the other person about the idea? Of course. Would you get buy-in? Maybe. Maybe not. A variety of factors could determine that. But let's suppose you do.

How many slides were required to explain your ideas? Probably none. You might draw a picture on a napkin or piece of paper, if needed, but you would simply carry on a conversation.

Let's suppose you're successful and receive approval to proceed. Then the person says: "I'd like you to talk to the rest of our group about this idea. There are implications across our organization that I'd like them to be aware of."

You might draw a picture on a napkin or piece of paper, if needed.

You learn that the group is composed of about ten people. They'll arrange a meeting time and find a room. They're prepared to give you forty-five minutes on their agenda. Thus, you'll have more time to speak to ten people than you had to talk to one.

How many visual aids will you use now? If you're like most people, you will sit down at your computer, open a slideware program, click your mouse, and begin organizing your ideas. But once you start using the technology, it's tough to stop. First you include a few pictures. Then there are charts. By the time you're done, even your notes are projected onto the screen or printed to paper.

But enough about you. Let's talk about the audience. Specifically, let's talk about your lunch partner and examine how he or she assimilates information. How does the way that person receives information orally suddenly change from when he or she listened to you in conversation, to when they are part of a small group, listening to you talk about the same concept with hopefully the same anticipated outcome?

The way your lunch partner takes in information doesn't change. You do. But should you? No, especially if you want to achieve the same outcome with the group that you achieved one-on-one. If you draw a picture for your lunch partner to explain your idea, it makes sense that you follow a similar process and draw a similar picture for the group.

As soon as you project your slides or refer to the presentation deck, of which everyone has a copy, you are asking people to read and listen at the same time. Most of us, instinctively or through experience, know that human beings cannot read and listen at the same time. If your spouse is talking to you and expects you to listen while you're reading the newspaper, you have a choice. You can continue reading the newspaper, or you can listen to your spouse. Interestingly, the science is becoming increasingly clear. If you try to read the newspaper and listen (even if both activities involve the same news item), you actually receive less than if you focus on only one or the other.[i]

Human beings cannot read and listen
at the same time.

The same applies to the evening news, because you can't think and listen at the same time. If your spouse is talking to you while you're attempting to watch the news item for the first time, you again have a choice. Pick one or the other. If you try to listen to both your spouse and the news item, you get virtually nothing from either.

In our working lunch example, your partner is going from a conversation over soup and sandwiches to being asked to read and listen at the same time. More importantly, the other nine people—who don't have the benefit of the conversation over lunch—are also being asked to read and listen at the same time. The result? They retain less information than if they conduct each activity separately.

You often see this when someone presents to a group with an anticipated outcome of getting a decision, such as budget approval. It may even occur when the decision at the meeting is simply a formality. The logic is boiled down to a deck of slides. The deck is perfect, but the decision is tabled.

Later, the presenter has a five-minute conversation with each decision maker. At the next meeting, the budget is approved without second thought. There are many people who have experienced this who now sell their ideas in advance. It's a good strategy, but it's time consuming. Wouldn't it be more productive to have the conversation with everyone at once and get a decision at the meeting?

Of course it would. But until we understand the value of separating orality from literacy—the spoken word from the written word—and conduct the same conversation with the group that is conducted one-on-one, preselling the budget will always be a good idea.

Underlying Assumptions

Let's imagine that I'm an extraterrestrial who is beamed from another planet to the seat beside you at a group meeting. The information is projected onto a screen at the front of the room and printed on paper in front of us. Suppose I lean over to you and ask: "Why is the speaker doing it this way? Why isn't he or she just talking to us?"

How would you reply?

They tell me they have to use slides because everyone uses slides.

Over the past twenty years, I've asked this question thousands of times. Almost everyone has the same two top assumptions—whether they are physicians, dentists, engineers, lawyers, not-for-profit executives, financial advisors, fund raisers, actuaries, accountants, consultants, public relations professionals, payroll professionals, career counselors, educators, administrators, bureaucrats, boards of directors, or others. They tell me they have to use slides because everyone uses slides. They also tell me that everyone expects them to use slides.

Over the years, I've identified ten basic assumptions around the use of slides in face-to-face communication, situations in which people knowingly mix the spoken word and the written word by projecting, printing, or both. You might state these assumptions a bit differently from what is written here, or you may add one or two assumptions to the list, but chances are you won't fundamentally disagree with them. You've probably heard, used, or assumed them all.

Assumption #1: Everyone Uses It

This assumption is the ultimate expression of "might makes right". Many people say that "everyone does it" when it comes to projectors and printed decks. But if we were examining this assumption in a critical thinking class at a first-year college or university, we would examine the fragile logic of:

- Everyone uses PowerPoint.
- I am part of everyone.
- Therefore, I must use PowerPoint too.

And it happens over and over again. Audience members walk out of a presentation with their eyes glazed; they start their computers and begin putting the deck together for their next presentation.

To break away from an overdependence on slides, we have to recognize two things. First, it's important to gain insights on how to effectively prepare without developing your content by sitting at a slideware program like PowerPoint or Keynote. If you use slides at all, they should be the last thing you develop—not the first.

Second, it's important to separate the spoken word and the written word—orality and literacy—that are two traditions of communication we've had for thousands of years. And those two forms have not changed. Every form of communication we have today can be categorized as either orality or literacy, regardless of the medium by which it's delivered to the audience.

The spoken word thrives in an environment of storytelling.

The spoken word thrives in an environment of storytelling. To tell stories well, we use words to create images, contrasts, and comparisons in the minds of audiences. By listening and being given the time to listen (which is something we'll discuss later), the receivers of information can use working memory and long-term memory together. They see themselves in the story that unfolds. And that's when communication works.

If properly used and applied, the spoken word is excellent at inspiring people. But it's a poor way to transmit data. Orality is an excellent way to exchange ideas, as long as that exchange is encouraged and permitted. Over lunch, you would never announce: "I'm buying, so I'm going to take fifteen minutes to talk about my idea. Then I'll save a few minutes at the end for questions." In a one-on-one conversation, questions are asked and answered throughout. Why can't we do the same with our presentations?

Literacy is the written word. It's a completely different form of communication. When we write something down, we capture the idea in time and space. Ideas can be built upon each other; knowledge can grow as future readers add their perspective, experience, and insights. Literacy is where data thrives. Without it, we would never have constructed the society in which we all live. If we still passed information from one generation to the next exclusively through the spoken word, we certainly wouldn't have the pool of knowledge necessary to build today's complex machines, laptop computers, or LCD projectors.

We've long had the ability to combine oral and written language.

As human beings, we've long had the ability to combine oral and written language. If bullet points can be printed as a presentation deck, why can't they just as easily be transcribed onto papyrus or carved onto stone tablets? This begs an important question: If we've had the ability to mix orality and literacy for centuries, why haven't we done so?

It's an interesting question. Part of the reason probably lies with the fact that it's now too easy to bring orality and literacy together; it's virtually mindless to create a presentation deck of printed slides. Tap out your bullet points and you're good to go. But I also believe we avoided mixing them because we knew it wouldn't work. And it doesn't. When I started my communications career in June 1982, it was a cardinal rule that you never provided the audience with your handouts at the start of your presentation. We knew they would read and stop listening.

Today, that rule is ignored everywhere. Now the handout can be on the screen and in front of each audience member at the same time. What is it about the evolutionary process that, in the five thousand years prior to the start of my career, we knew that human beings couldn't read and listen at the same time, yet magically and mysteriously we now think they can?

If you want to be more effective, you must separate the spoken word and the written word—regardless of whether you're the sender or the receiver in the communication process. If your investment advisor insists on walking you through an investment plan, ignore the written words and focus on what the advisor is saying, no matter how many times he or she points to the document. Likewise, if you're an investment advisor, don't walk your clients through the plan. Send it in advance of the meeting or provide it as a handout when the meeting has concluded. When you get together, carry on a structured conversation and answer client questions clearly and concisely.

A large part of the problem with modern presentations is that we try to transmit large amounts of data, rather than telling the story behind the data. To communicate effectively, you should strive to understand the value of each method of communication (spoken vs. written word), capitalize on the strengths of each, and—most importantly—separate them.

> *Minimize not only the number of slides*
> *but also what's on each slide.*

If you project your slides or deliver from a deck (and that's a very large "if"), minimize not only the number of slides but also what's on each slide. Use your slides as section headers. Eliminate bullet points. If you need a chart, graph, or picture, use it—but only if it will add value. And when you no longer need it, remove it from view.

Assumption #2: It's Expected

It's difficult to determine where "everyone does it" ends and "it's expected" begins. People often say they have to use PowerPoint because the audience expects them to. But who expects it? And why?

Imagine you work for a mutual fund company. Your firm is introducing a new product and they have sent you a PowerPoint presentation as the basis for the sales presentations to investment advisors in your region. The business goal is to motivate advisors to place their clients' money into your new product.

Do you deliver the presentation? Of course. If the marketing department didn't want you to do so, they wouldn't have prepared it in the first place. It's an expectation. And that expectation has been around since laser printers became close and personal with acetate overheads.

From 1996 to 2003, when our son was growing up, I coached competitive baseball. Early in my coaching career, I decided to pursue coaching certification, partly because it was encouraged and partly because it was an opportunity to be exposed to different training styles as a form of professional development for my career.

Each level of certification had three stages: theory, technical, and practical. Theory and technical levels are provided during weekend workshops. The practical stage verifies coaching experience, usually one season of coaching per level.

For my level one theory, I attended a weekend workshop at a local college. To this day, I believe it was the longest six weeks I have ever spent in a two-day workshop. For the majority of the two-day program, the instructor stood at the front of the room and marched through her overhead transparencies (reading many of them aloud) so the class could follow along. The overheads had been prepared by the leadership of the coaching certification program. I guess the logic was that they expected her to use the overheads, or they wouldn't have prepared them in the first place. I don't usually get headaches, but it took nearly three days for me to get rid of that one.

The next year, for my level two theory, I drove to the other side of the city, even though I could have attended a workshop near my home. Level two was conducted Friday evening, plus all day Saturday and Sunday. Because of traffic, I left home at 4:30 p.m. to arrive for a 7:00 p.m. start. I barely made it.

But I was glad I did. The first thing the facilitator did was put the overhead projector into a corner, saying: "We won't need that this weekend." I breathed a sigh of relief.

During the next two-and-a-half days, he created an intense and fulfilling learning environment, using a variety of techniques to enhance our understanding. Discussion began as soon as the workshop started and carried on throughout. We shared experiences with each other, enabling all of us to learn from everyone else. The facilitator easily answered more than one thousand questions himself.

I left the workshop thinking I couldn't wait for the baseball season to start. Attending that workshop helped me become a better coach—and a better consultant. To this day, I use a number of tools and techniques I learned that weekend.

Today's audiences should be easy to please;
they don't want to be bored.

When it comes to expectations for presentations, today's audiences should be easy to please. First and foremost, they don't want to be bored. They don't like to waste their time. I have yet to meet anyone who attends a presentation thinking: "I wonder what colors the presenter will use," or "I hope the slides are engaging."

In future, I hope audiences will expect information for the presentations they attend to be tailored to their specific needs, not pulled off a shelf and presented without second thought. I hope audiences will expect the presenter to understand not only who they are on the outside but also to gain insight into their interests, beliefs, attitudes, and opinions. Audiences of the future will demand value from their decision to attend a presentation. Value is not created by the data; it's the *how* and *why* behind the data. Why is this important to the audience? How will this help them?

In the future, I hope audiences will expect a conversation. If written information is needed to start the conversation, smart audiences will want that information in advance. Audiences will want time to read it and will want presenters to assume that they have. They will not want to plod through the same written information when everyone gets together. Smart audiences will want visuals only where needed. They will want the opportunity to probe by asking questions. During precious "face time," they will want information put into perspective, not have data driven down their throats.

Assumption #3: People Have Different Learning Styles

The underlying assumption here is that a lot of people are visual learners. Ergo, they need slides to help them learn.

This assumption is loosely based on research around the concept of neurolinguistic programming. Although neurolinguistic programming had a controversial start in the 1970s, it has found a home in training, education, and coaching. The logic is that if you understand how people absorb information (an athlete, for example), you can feed that need and enhance their ability to process and learn from it.

There are three basic learning styles: visual, auditory, and kinesthetic. In theory, each of us has a dominant learning style, although we can and do apply all three. When coaching athletes, you tell them, you show them (and also have them visualize it), and then have them practice it over and over again. I have never seen statistics on how many of us there are in visual, auditory, or kinesthetic categories. But in rooms of ten people or more, I've never had difficulty finding all three.

To determine someone's dominant learning style, ask them a question and watch their eyes while they're thinking. If they look up to form their answer, they tend to be visual learners. If their eyes go from side to side while thinking, they tend to be auditory learners, which includes both listening and reading, because they create a voice in their heads when reading words. If they look down, they tend to be kinesthetic learners. They learn best by doing.

When people question learning styles and visual aids, they tend to believe that slides are good for visual learners. If that's the case, what about auditory and kinesthetic learners? Don't they count? Why aren't they included? But this is actually a fallacy. The vast majority of slides are simply words written on paper or projected onto a screen. Therefore, most presentations are designed to meet the needs of auditory learners, who learn well by reading.

For me, the best way to examine different learning styles is to think of giving someone directions. Visual learners can't follow directions without creating a visual map in their head. And it's important to recognize that this map has to be in their head, not yours. If they create that map and you point them northward, chances are they'll get there.

Auditory learners don't necessarily need to know which direction is north. Point them in a direction and provide fairly specific instructions. For example, tell them to go six blocks and turn left, turn right at the service station, or keep to the right after they pass the hospital. If the directions are specific and remembered, they'll probably get there.

We can all participate as senders and receivers during conversations.

Kinesthetic learners are a different breed. The only thing more difficult than giving them directions is getting directions from them. Kinesthetic learners have trouble getting there, but (and this is my own discovery, based on the number of times this issue has come up in my workshops) once they get there, the route is etched in their memory. They probably never have to ask for directions or consult a map again—even years later.

But the interesting thing about neurolinguistic programming is that, regardless of our primary learning style, we can all participate as senders and receivers during conversations. Every member of every audience you've ever addressed, regardless of each individual's learning style, can process information effectively when it's received conversationally, which enables them to process your ideas in ways that are best for them. My advice? Find your conversational style and develop it, and you will communicate more effectively with groups large and small.

Assumption #4: A Picture is Worth a Thousand Words

This may be true, but only under specific circumstances. First, the slide must be a picture, not words. A picture of six words by six lines is thirty-six words. Mathematically, it is 964 words short of a thousand. Most slides are not pictures. They are words. The next time you look at a presentation deck of printed slides, ask yourself how many are pictures and how many are words.

Second, limit the number of graphs and charts you use. We've all sat through presentations of charts and graphs presented in what seems like an unending sequence. If those don't create a headache, nothing will.

Third, photographs and artist renderings must be sparingly used. Some people eliminate bullet points from their presentations in favor of projecting a series of pictures to help tell the story. The intent is good, but often, they end up with too many pictures.

*Successful presentations feed
this internal creation process.*

I've tested this when speaking to groups after someone has applied this tactic. Interestingly, if you ask audience members to describe the pictures they remember, they can usually only describe one or two correctly, especially if they were exposed to many. Often, they describe pictures that were not actually shown as part of the presentation. They listen to the speaker and create their own pictures in their head.

This has led me to an important conclusion. If a picture a presenter shows is worth a thousand words, the picture each audience member creates in his or her mind from the stories told are worth ten thousand more. Successful presentations feed this internal creation process. And that's when communication truly works.

Assumption #5: My Slides Are My Notes

This is an assumption that can trace its roots to the vertical format of acetate overheads. These are the infamous bullet points.

You will often hear people say: "I use my bullet points as notes and talk to my points," or "I talk to my slides." I've heard variations of this phrase for the better part of twenty years. Every time I hear it, I have to stop myself before I ask: "Do your bullet points ever respond? Do they ever ask questions? Do they apply your information or take action on it?"

Think about it. "I talk to my bullet points." "I talk to my slides." These expressions create an image of a barrier between sender and receiver in the communication process. And that's exactly what happens.

The speaker looks often at the slides. The audience, of course, does the same. This is a distraction because the focus is removed from the person doing the talking. In face-to-face communication, it's better for the receiver to be looking at the person speaking. This is why talking to someone in person has incremental value over talking to the same person about the same thing via telephone. Try having a conversation with a family member if he or she is distracted and not looking at you when you're sharing information with them.

Now, does that mean you should never use notes during your presentations? Absolutely not. (We'll talk about that later.) However, if you think you're increasing your effectiveness by putting your notes in front of the audience, either projected or as a printed deck, you're fooling yourself. Forget the six-by-six rule of six lines per slide with six words per line, unless those notes are for you, and your audience cannot see them. Even Microsoft knows this, which is why it published *Beyond Bullet Points*.

I have never seen a speaker improve
by projecting notes onto a screen.

But here's another observation I'd like to share. During nearly twenty years of presentation training, I have never seen a speaker improve by projecting notes onto a screen or printing them onto a deck and delivering the same information the audience can read. At my workshops, many people have challenged that concept over the years, so I video record them delivering a presentation their way (with notes on the screen) and my way (where the audience can't see the notes). Then I play back both recordings without interruption. Nobody improves. Ever. In fact, they watch uncomfortably as their skills deteriorate during the first method and immediately improve during the second.

Assumption #6: The Audience Can Take Notes

The intent of this assumption is good, but the practical application often leaves much to be desired. And the reality is that thousands of trees are killed each day in the name of allowing people the opportunity to take notes.

When you ask people to show you the notes they've taken on the printed presentation decks they've received, there are usually a few at the very beginning, then virtually nothing throughout the remainder of the handout. I recently participated in a web seminar that was organized by a professional association to which I belong. The web seminar was free and evolved as a result of a five-month discussion that took place on the association's LinkedIn site under the heading: "How many communicators still use PowerPoint? If you do, why? If you don't, what are you using instead?" After more than a hundred responses over a five-month period, the president of the association informed us that they would be conducting a free web seminar on the use of PowerPoint.

Great, I thought to myself; the organization is listening. My expectation was that we would have a robust discussion on whether PowerPoint should be used at all, especially since the president of the association had stated on the discussion thread that she rarely uses the program, if at all, and she's an excellent speaker.

What we got was someone who makes his living by putting the finishing touches on slides for others. So much for the robust discussion on whether to use the program; his ability to feed himself depends on it. He then told us that he is the last person in the chain of events prior to the speech or presentation. Wonderful. I guess that means we won't be having a discussion of strategic communication. Strategic thinking has long since ended by the time he is contacted. Finally, he told us that if we have any questions, we could e-mail him after the presentation. Perfect. Another one-way transmission of information. Oh well, it was free. The association's heart was in the right place.

The handout, which was sent in advance, was forty slides in length, but only fourteen pages because the .pdf file was organized as three slides per page. I printed it and took some notes. Actually, I took two or three notes on the first page, and then worked on other things for most of the remainder of the one-and-one-half hours while the presentation droned on in the background.

I would have preferred a discussion of whether to use the program at all.

Personally, I would have preferred a discussion of whether to use the program at all. The person conducting the web seminar told us that he rarely sees his work. Perhaps his impression of the value of his work would change if he sat through a couple dozen of the presentations he helped put together. It would be interesting to see if his perspective changes after viewing slides from the receiver's perspective, which is really the only perspective that counts.

Assumption #7: They Can Share the Presentation with Others
The assumption here is that people can share the deck, and others can get the point. Think about that for a moment: If someone can read your information and understand your ideas without you there, then why are you there?

In 1997, I attended the level one technical workshop for my coaching certification. Unlike theory workshops that include all sports, the technical workshop is sport specific. In my case, it was baseball.

The facilitator's job was to help us better understand throwing, catching, hitting, and running so we can then teach these concepts to our athletes. He used a ball, a bat, a base, and a glove to demonstrate a number of concepts. Technically, each of these is a visual aid. We pushed desks and chairs to the side of the room, and he created a mini baseball diamond. People sitting on chairs represented the bases. People standing represented position players.

We covered strategies for offense and defense. He had a volunteer demonstrate proper finishing positions for bent leg slides and hook slides. He showed us how to properly hold a bat by gripping our index finger along our calluses, rather than the middle of our palms.

He provided an excellent handout. We didn't even open it during the day, but I referred to it frequently throughout my coaching career. The booklet followed the major headings he covered during the workshop, and I could have learned quite a bit by reading it in isolation. But I never could have received the richness of the in-person experience by reading the handout alone.

Assumption #8: People Will Remember Our Key Messages

I have been a member of the public relations and communication management industry for thirty years. My profession coined the term "key messages," but it's a phrase I could just as soon do without. The reason? It implies that success occurs when someone can remember the key messages, rather than apply the information the messages contain or take action on them. Emphasizing key messages focuses on communication inputs, rather than seeking appropriate attitudinal or behavioral outcomes. In other words, the mistaken perception is that the more you hammer home your key messages, the more effective they become.

In business presentations,
you want one of two outcomes.

In business presentations, you want one of two outcomes. In an informative presentation, you want people to apply your information. "I'm giving you this information so you can apply it to your decision-making process," or "I hope you'll have a better understanding of how our project fits into the overall strategy we're pursuing as an organization, so you can better manage your own projects." In a persuasive presentation, you want people to take direct and immediate action, i.e. book an appointment, sign a petition, create a bylaw, vote a certain way, or contact their elected official. Effective communication is about outcomes, not inputs. Did they apply our information? Did they take the action we suggested?

Key messages are never an end unto themselves. People who focus on key messages often fall prey to the implied assumption that if they repeat their messages long enough and often enough, they'll get the outcomes they're seeking—but this is not necessarily true.

The best way I've found to explain this is to ask people how many times they have asked their children to turn off the light in their room. If you're like most of us, the answer is: "Too many to count." Yet turning the light off is an excellent key message. It's based in economic reality and environmental sensitivity. Today's children are exposed to information about the environment that should make it easy for them to connect turning off the light in their room to saving the planet. But repeating the key message simply does not work.

To get the outcomes you're seeking, sometimes it's important to change the input. This is what I learned with our son.

Every May, when he comes home from university and leaves the light on in his room, I call out to him and ask him to please come upstairs and turn it off. "But dad, you're right there," he will say.

"Yes," I reply, "but I'm not the one who left it on."

He will then have to unwind his six-foot-seven-inch frame from in front of the television, where he's watching sports-something, walk up the stairs, and turn off the light in his room. It usually only takes once or twice before he modifies his own behavior, and I never have to ask again—at least until the next time he comes home!

Remembering key messages is unimportant in communication.

Remembering key messages is unimportant in communication. Applying information or taking action counts for everything. If someone applies your information to their decision-making process or takes action on it, key messages are, by definition, remembered. And you shouldn't need to beat people over the head to achieve that goal.

Assumption #9: The Focus is Off Me

Someone who expresses this assumption is usually nervous about delivering presentations to others. But there are a couple of difficulties with this assumption. The first is that using slides in presentations has led us to the point where we have put presentations on a pedestal. As Edward Tufte points out in *The Cognitive Style of PowerPoint*, the modern presentation style puts the speaker in a power relationship with the audience. In my experience, this increases nervousness.

But the reality is that in conversations of all types, the person receiving the information should be looking at the person sending it. When you're engaged in conversation, whether with one person or a group, you want the audience to look at you.

This is something I've demonstrated many times during my workshops. I ask for a volunteer from the audience. It's an easy role; the person doesn't even have to move. I ask the person to stare at a blank screen or flip chart at the front of the room. They keep their eyes on that blank image while we have a conversation.

I stand at the left side of the screen and point out that some advice says the speaker should be on the left-hand side of their slides. The logic is that people's eyes go from left to right. Then I move to the right-hand side. I point out that if someone was delivering a presentation in the Middle East, they would need to be on that side because the eye goes from right to left. Of course, if delivering a presentation in China or Japan, it would be important to be at the top of the screen because writing goes from top to bottom.

But I usually deliver my presentations in western-based nations, so I move back to the left-hand side and talk to my volunteer directly. Throughout this, their eyes have remained on the screen. I inform my volunteer that the two of us are now going to have a conversation and ask if he or she is comfortable.

Sometimes I have to ask a couple of times because a person has trouble listening while their eyes are on the screen. Then I ask:

"Do you feel more or less connected to the communication process than if you were looking at me?"

"Much less connected," they always reply.

> *A blank screen got in the way of the most*
> *powerful form of communication.*

I tell them they no longer need to keep their eyes on the screen. I point out that the screen contained no charts, no graphs, no bullet points, no paragraphs, no quotes, no pictures, no illustrations, and no spinning logo. A blank screen got in the way of the most powerful form of communication we have as human beings. Imagine what PowerPoint, Keynote or Prezi can do if you truly unleash their potential. Charts, graphs, pictures, and words are much more compelling—and thereby much more distracting—than a blank screen.

Assumption #10: It Saves Time

I cannot believe that people actually say this. But they do. If you've ever assembled a presentation using PowerPoint, Keynote, or Prezi, you know that it can absolutely suck up your time. The U.S. Armed Forces coined a term for junior officers who spend most of their time developing presentation decks: PowerPoint Rangers.[ii]

I've heard of instances in which two professionals spent more than two hundred hours assembling a 150-slide deck for a presentation to an organization's board of directors. This doesn't seem to be saving a lot of time.

Let's put a value on that by assuming these two professionals each earn 125 thousand dollars per year. With benefits, the cost to the organization is about eighty-five dollars per hour each. Multiply that by two hundred hours, and you have seventeen thousand dollars in salary and benefits for one single deck.

But enough about the cost of putting such presentations together. Let's talk about the cost of delivering them.

My wife and I had friends over for dinner recently. One of the people who visited us is a sales manager for a large brokerage firm. That week, he had attended a three-day sales conference for his organization. For the majority of the three days, he was subjected to PowerPoint presentation after PowerPoint presentation. By the afternoon break on the third day, he retained virtually nothing. It all blended together.

When the group reassembled for the home stretch, the room had been changed. No more big screen for PowerPoint. There was a stool in the middle of the stage and a microphone on the stool. My friend said there was an audible sigh of relief from his peers. The speaker sat on the stool and had a conversation with the fifty people in the room. He recapped the highlights of the three days and answered questions.

They all wondered why they didn't just have that session.

Two things were discussed when the session concluded. First, everyone talked about how effective this radical departure from the norm actually was. Second, they all wondered why they didn't have just that session.

Again, let's put an actual value on this. Each of the sales managers makes a minimum of two hundred thousand dollars per year. With benefits, it's about $125 per hour. In salaries alone, the cost to the organization for a three-day sales conference easily exceeds $150,000, plus travel and conference-related expenses. There is also the productivity loss of not having them actually do their jobs for those three days.

Yes, I know you're thinking about all kinds of objections right now. They had to come together. Networking was important. We had to deliver our key messages. How can you have a conference without PowerPoint? And so on.

But if you have the courage to test your convictions, I recommend that the next time you organize such a conference, ask participants to complete a twenty-five-question, multiple-choice quiz at the end of the third day, and base it on information contained in the presentations that were delivered via PowerPoint.

At the next conference, ban PowerPoint or limit each speaker to two slides.

Encourage speakers to have conversations with their audiences, and then ask participants to complete a twenty-five-question quiz based on the information covered during those workshops. Compare the scores from the two quizzes and make plans for your next conference.

Where To From Here?

Albert Einstein once said that the definition of insanity is doing the same thing over and over again and expecting different results. We're at a stage in the information age where millions of people around the world use slides without giving second thought to whether what they're doing is actually working. It isn't, or the expression 'Death by PowerPoint' would never have been coined. For every presentation that uses slides well, it's easy to find dozens that don't.

"That's the way it's done"
is no longer good enough.

It's now time to admit that "that's the way it's done" is no longer good enough. But don't take my word for it. The sad fact is that there's virtually no academic, peer-reviewed research to determine if slides work, when they work, or why. In preparation for a master's thesis in 2007, author Robert Lane wrote:

"Considering digital presentation's established history and widespread use, we expected to find that the cognitive effects of, and best practices for, PowerPoint-style communication had been well-studied. We certainly were shocked to find the opposite was true. Other than a handful of limited exceptions, researchers apparently have utterly ignored this vast slice of human communication, leaving an untold number of important issues and questions unexplored. As far as we can tell, hundreds of millions of speakers regularly follow various protocols and precedents for presentation design and delivery, with virtually no published validation of any kind to explain what works, when, why, and with whom."[iii]

It's time to face reality; the emperor has no clothes, and slides are not working. They stifle discussion. They impede understanding. They hinder decision making. They crush audience participation. They smother critical thinking. They leave boredom and lost productivity in their wake. Yet millions of people the world over continue producing and using them on a daily basis. I wonder if this is what Einstein had in mind when he left us his lucid definition.

If you search "death by powerpoint" on the Internet, you'll find all kinds of advice on how to deal with the problem. Virtually all this advice still clings, unfortunately, to the underlying assumption that slides are essential. In the 2011 version of his "Annoying PowerPoint" survey, appropriately located at his PowerPoint blog, a consultant tells us that his research shows that nearly one-fifth of people view one presentation per day, a significant increase over the past few years. "Presentations are becoming a more common way of communicating in organizations," he writes. However, "the quality of presentations doesn't seem to be getting better." Of course not. If you cling to the premise that slides are essential and you keep using slides, you're going to keep getting the same results. If you develop content while sitting at PowerPoint (or any other slideware program), be prepared to limit your success.

We must get off this treadmill completely if we hope to improve communication. To do that, we have to recognize that the best way to communicate face-to-face is by absolutely minimizing slides, if they're used at all, and that it's no longer good enough to exchange one treadmill for another. For example, there's a "new" form of presentation making the rounds called pecha kucha that originated in Tokyo in 2003 as an evening in which young designers could meet, network, and show their work in public. Drawing its name from the Japanese term for *chitchat*, this format is based on showing twenty images for twenty seconds each. You set the timing on your slide program and talk for twenty seconds as each slide is shown on-screen. In theory, it makes presentations concise and keeps things moving. While pecha kucha has the potential of reducing boredom to six-minute-forty-second bites, it's another example of the medium dictating the message. It's a one-way transmission of information, not communication. As such, it may be good for networking designers, but it has absolutely no place in the boardroom, the meeting room, the conference room, the training room, the classroom, or in any form of sales presentation.

Stepping off the PowerPoint treadmill
requires courage.

Stepping off the PowerPoint treadmill requires courage. It requires intestinal fortitude to stop running for the cliff when everyone around you can't wait to jump. But if you're interested in setting yourself apart and enhancing your results, this book is here to help you. By embracing these five steps, your ability to communicate effectively will improve as you:

1. Put your audience first
2. Structure the conversation
3. Minimize visual aids
4. Convey your message and personality
5. Answer questions throughout

The first two steps accompany the workbook that is available at www. FiveStepsToConquer.com. The workbook is free. You can download it and use it to develop every presentation you'll deliver in the future. By using the book and workbook together to prepare presentations, you'll gain models for understanding the audiences to whom you're presenting. You'll focus on matching their needs to your insight and knowledge. You'll learn to develop a Strategic Approach for every presentation.

Your content will improve because The Basic Presentation Framework will teach you to structure clear, concise conversations with all audiences, whether you're engaging one-on-one in sales calls or presenting your ideas to thousands. Better yet, you'll save time because you won't spend endless hours messing around with slides.

Step Three, Step Four and *Step Five* focus on helping you enhance the delivery of your material. As you read through them, you'll understand why it's important to minimize visual aids, but you'll also be empowered to use a variety of tools to help you communicate effectively. You'll gain insight into the value of conveying your message and personality. As you do, your conversational skills will improve—regardless of whether you're talking to one person or a thousand. Finally, *Step Five* helps ensure that your audiences are engaged because they'll have the ability to ask questions about your information at any time.

But enough about you. Let's turn the five steps around and examine them from the audience's perspective. At the end of the day, this is the only perspective that counts. For them, the logic of this book is irrefutable. What audience wouldn't like their needs placed first? If you were a member of an audience and you had a choice between participating in a structured conversation and sitting through a presentation, which would you pick? The conversation implies engagement and participation. The presentation summons images of bullet points and boredom.

When it comes to visuals, how often have you heard someone comment: "Gosh, I wish the presenter used more slides," or "Gee, I don't think thirty-five slides were nearly enough"? How many audiences demand that their questions be kept until the end of the presentation, assuming there's time left? Or would they prefer their questions to be answered throughout in a more conversational and engaging format?

Stop the tail from wagging the dog.

At no point in this book will you read that "visuals are not important" or "slides should not be used." However, the overriding purpose of this book is to stop the tail from wagging the dog. Visuals should be an aid, not a crutch. They should be a spice, not the meal. They should support communication, not dictate it. They should be one tool, not the only tool. They should be developed at the end of the content development process, not the beginning.

As you finish this book, you'll gain renewed insight into how to communicate effectively with others. If we can accomplish that simple yet monumental task together—facilitating better engagement and better communication during those increasingly rare opportunities when people get together—we'll make better use of everyone's time and ultimately generate better results. Join me in this quest. Together, we can change the world, one conversation at a time.

Step One:
Put Your Audience First

You're still reading, but you're probably a bit confused. Sure, you buy into some of the concepts discussed in the previous chapter, but how can you deliver a presentation without slides or a printed presentation deck of some kind? What's the alternative?

But let's be absolutely clear here. If you truly wish to stop glazing the eyes of people who give up their valuable time to listen to you, you should not use PowerPoint or Keynote or Prezi or SlideRocket or any other slideware program to develop your content. That's not the purpose for which it was designed. If you develop slides, do so only after you've established your strategy—*after* you've considered the audience, established business and communication objectives, and structured your side of the conversation. Until you do that, leave your slideware program closed.

Slideware was created to mimic the horizontal format of 35-mm slides at a time when 35-mm computer-generated slides cost anywhere from thirty-five to seventy-five dollars each on the open market. I worked on a college field placement in late 1981, where slides for a series of employee meetings were ordered at a cost of seventy-five dollars apiece. Today, accounting for the change in the value of a dollar, those slides would cost at least two hundred fifty dollars each. If someone had to find twenty-seven hundred dollars in his or her budget for a thirty-six slide presentation to an internal sales conference or monthly management meeting, no one would worry about being exposed to too many slides.

Today, projectors and printers are everywhere. Slides are "free," and slideware programs have become slide factories. But slides have never been effective at developing content; what's actually killing us is the act of opening, pointing, clicking, and typing. The presentation itself is merely the visible result of a flawed critical thinking process.

*Slides are "free" and slideware programs
have become slide factories.*

Two-Way Symmetrical Communication

In research associated with the communication profession, there is a well-recognized model known as two-way symmetrical communication. One of the defining features of this model is the desire to create win-win outcomes. Both sides seek to gain from the exchange.[iv]

Two-way symmetrical communication improves understanding and builds better relationships. Research has shown that, in large part, this model is ultimately more effective, because it puts equal emphasis on both sender and receiver in the communication process.[v] In other words, the person or group receiving the information is just as important as the person or group sending it.

The vast majority of today's business presentations are barely two-way and are anything but symmetrical. There is virtually no equality between sender and receiver. Every time a presenter says "we'll try to save some time at the end for questions," the implication is that the audience is the least important. This leaves us in a state of affairs where information has become more important than the understanding it is supposed to generate. To create effective understanding, exactly the opposite needs to be true.

How much of this unequal relationship between sender and receiver is caused by too many slides? In his booklet, *The Cognitive Style of PowerPoint,* Professor Edward Tufte outlines his belief that an overreliance on slides reduces participation. Dr. Tufte believes that computer-generated graphics establish a dominance relationship between speaker and audience. He likens slide-driven presentations to military parades in Stalin Square. This comparison may be a bit over the top, but it begs an important question. Does the average presenter's reliance on slides—whether projected or printed or both—add to the information sharing process or impede it?

People will likely argue both sides of this question for many years to come, even after the publication of this book. But the reality at the end of the argument is that a phrase like 'Death by PowerPoint' does not create an image of a conversation or an engaged audience. It does not create an image of symmetry. It leaves the impression that one side in the communication process has become more important, and it is ultimately boring the other to death.

Members of the audience
are the most important people in the room.

As a theoretical model, two-way symmetrical communication is the foundation on which win-win outcomes can be constructed, but let's be clear. Members of the audience, not the presenter, are the most important people in the room. Without them, the presentation is as useful as a monologue in front of a mirror, perhaps interesting to the presenter but relatively useless to the audience.

The audience must come first. If what you're saying is inconsistent with their expectations as they walk in to the presentation, they'll simply stop listening. If the audience doesn't buy in or, as a bare minimum, understand what you're talking about, you've wasted their time. More importantly, you've wasted yours.

You must consider audience needs first. You want your win, to be sure. You want strategic gain from your presentations, whether to inform or persuade. But your win is inextricably linked to the audience's need for information and the value they receive from listening to you. Where are the specific points at which their need for information matches what you can provide? These focal points need to shape the strategic direction of every presentation you deliver.

The purpose of this chapter is to enhance your critical thinking skills and improve your strategic perspective. The goal is to provide a foundation on which you can develop and deliver more effective presentations that put audience needs first and lead to win-win outcomes. The audience wins because they gain value from listening to you and participating in your presentation. You win by advancing your personal and/or professional objectives. The bridge between these wins is the point at which portions of your knowledge best meet the needs of that specific audience. And every audience is different.

To help you construct this bridge effectively, a workbook has been created to help you work through this step and *Step Two: Structure the Conversation.*

The workbook outlines a step-by-step process to help you develop effective presentations, including a series of models and frameworks to assist you. You can download a free .pdf version of the workbook at www.FiveStepsToConquer.com.

For every presentation you develop in the future, your goal is to develop a Strategic Approach similar to the example at the end of this chapter. You also need to develop a Basic Presentation Framework and a comprehensive notes outline, similar to the example in *Step Two*. The workbook is there to assist you. Please use it to structure all future presentations.

Define the Need

The first component of developing a successful presentation is to define and understand the underlying need or specific opportunity that exists with a specific audience at a particular moment in time. Focus is important to success. You achieve focus by matching what you hope to accomplish to what the audience needs to understand. Each group is fundamentally different. Increase your success at the start of the planning process by tapping into their need to understand, although this is not always the same as your perceived need to "tell."

This means asking a number of important questions. How can my information help them? Do my goals match theirs? If so, how specifically do they match? If not, what are the discrepancies, and how can I mitigate those discrepancies prior to going any further in the content development process?

Once you've identified the needs you'll address, write them down in four or five brief sentences. At this stage, use sentences, not bullet points. You should be able to hand these sentences to your boss or a colleague, who should then be able to understand exactly what you hope the audience will learn, know, or understand as a result of your presentation—but from their perspective to understand, not necessarily your desire to "tell." Focus your strategy. Keep each sentence as simple as possible.

Develop a Strategic Approach
for every presentation you deliver.

An example of how this can be done is in the Strategic Approach at the end of this chapter, which is a presentation to a municipal council on the need to develop a new "barking dog" bylaw. If you wish to increase your consistency and success, I encourage you to develop a Strategic Approach for every presentation you deliver.

Translate Need into Value

Translating the needs you've identified into value for the audience means putting yourself in the audience's shoes by asking: "If I were sitting in the audience, why would I give up my valuable time to attend this presentation? What do I gain by listening? What value will I receive? How will the information in this presentation help me?" As part of your Strategic Approach, write down the value you intend to provide in one or two short sentences.

At all times, your job is to turn mountains of data into usable pieces of a puzzle that can ultimately improve understanding and facilitate effective decision making. The best way to do this is to answer one (or both) of two important questions: How? Why? If someone from a sales-based organization presents quarterly results at a management meeting, the focus needs to be on answering "How?" and "Why?" for the audience: "How much are our sales up from last quarter? Why was there an increase? How is this relevant to our business? Why were our sales better in one region than another? How did one person or one group manage to sell more? Why does their experience differ from others? How can we capitalize on this trend?"

Too often in presentations, we assume that the audience will answer "How?" and "Why?" on their own when presented with the facts. This is not the case. Your job is to turn specific parts of your data into usable information from the audience's point of view. You must answer "How?" and "Why?" to make the data relevant. The value is the information they receive, not the data you transmit. This is not only a subtle distinction in communication effectiveness; it is a critical one.

Analyze the Audience

As a general rule, the better you understand the people who attend your presentations, the more successful you will be, provided that you apply that insight effectively to the challenge of matching what they need to hear with what you can tell them. Each audience has common characteristics. They have opinions about the messages or issues you will discuss. They're there for a reason. They don't want to waste their time.

There are two distinct levels used to define audiences.

You must do everything possible to tap into the similarities that each individual brings to the presentation and the characteristics they share as a group. Keep in mind that there are two distinct levels used to define audiences: demographic characteristics and shared opinions.

Demographic characteristics are the first way most people analyze an audience. This includes age, education level, cultural background, gender, and socio-economic status. Within any organization or group, there are a number of levels at which demographic distinctions can be made. The characteristics of those on the shop floor will differ from the board of directors. The characteristics of supervisors will differ from those of senior executives. By understanding people's basic demographic traits, you enhance your ability to shape information that will influence them.

A second method of analyzing the audience has less to do with their external demographic characteristics than with their internal opinions, attitudes, and beliefs. Communication research demonstrates that people can be grouped according to the opinions they share, often irrespective of demographic characteristics. The more narrowly you define this grouping, the better you can understand them and the more effectively you can communicate with them.

For example, let's suppose we're a school board, and we've decided to increase the school board portion of municipal taxes by 12 percent. We are now meeting with community groups to explain our decision. There is no doubt that people react to the issue.

There are three basic reactions to any issue. People will support your perspective with a positive opinion. People will oppose your perspective with a negative opinion. People will not care about your perspective (neutral opinion). Your job is to understand as much as possible about whether they have a positive, negative, or neutral opinion about your perspective and the underlying issues on which it's constructed, before tailoring your information accordingly.

With the school board example, we know that our decision will impact homeowners as direct taxpayers, and tenants as indirect taxpayers. But within each of these broad audience classifications, we can subdivide in other ways. For example:

- Homeowners with school-aged children.
- Homeowners with grown children.
- Homeowners with preschool children.
- Homeowners who are planning families.
- Homeowners who do not now—and likely will never—have children.

These are five distinct audiences within the broader homeowner category. Each has a potentially different reaction to this issue. There are similarities, but in some cases the reactions could be significantly different. And the reactions have little to do with demographics. For example, two families of four could be completely different from a demographic perspective, but be the same audience on the basis of shared opinions. The parents could be of a different age. Household income could be vastly different. One family could live in a house valued at over a million dollars. The other could live in a house valued at $250,000. On the basis of demographic characteristics, they could not be grouped together. But if each family has two children enrolled in the public school system, they will each react in a similar manner to the issue of a significant tax increase, and can therefore be grouped together as an audience. Each will be thinking: "What's in it for my kids? How will this improve their education?"

As a general statement, if members of the group are generally supportive of your message, your goal is to reinforce their opinion. Acknowledge their support and provide additional reasons for expanding or reinforcing that support. Structure your facts and stories in ways that provide these specific audiences with tools they need to continue to support your message and perhaps even argue your case long after you've left the room.

You won't be successful if you meet
their opposition head-on.

If members of the group are generally opposed to your message, it's important to acknowledge that they have a different perspective from yours. It is, after all, their right. Your goal should be to neutralize negative opinions, not necessarily change those opinions. In some cases, your win may be as basic as convincing the group as a whole to agree to disagree, or to not oppose your perspective.

When faced with a negative group, you won't be successful if you meet their opposition head-on. In fact, if you use this strategy, you will lose. They are probably closer to each other than they are to you, especially if their opinion is different from yours. By meeting them head-on, you create a "me versus them" environment in which they'll look to each other—and the similar opinions they hold—as sources of comfort. Provide your basic information, and then answer as many questions as humanly possible. Allow them to explore your logic. You may need to let vocal members of the group vent their frustration. And if there is real hostility in the room prior to your arrival, you should consider answering questions first and presenting your information later.

If members of the group don't have an opinion and basically couldn't care less, your job is to encourage them to formulate an opinion about your message and the issue it represents. In many ways, this is the most difficult challenge to overcome. After all, if nobody cares, how do you get them to care?

But with this type of presentation, you have a couple of important factors working for you. Everyone has decided to spend time listening to you. By nature, people will actively seek opportunities that make the best possible use of their time. As they listen, they will attempt to make your information relevant to themselves as individuals. Your job at this point is to facilitate that process by making everything you say directly relevant to their need to understand the value you're providing. Explain the value of your message, and then shape your facts and stories to convince them of its importance to them.

The more you understand your audience on the basis of demographics and shared opinions, the more effective you can be at tapping into what brings them all into that room at that particular time. By doing so, you create value with your message and provide information that's directly relevant to their needs, what they hold valuable, and what they hope to achieve as a group. This creates a strong foundation that can significantly enhance your success.

Understand the Event

Your final analysis is to understand the event that has brought the audience together. Very often, this is an important key to tapping into the common characteristics they possess as a group.

You need to ask some questions.

To do this, you need to ask some questions: Who else is presenting? What will they talk about? Is there a theme to the meeting? If so, what is it? How does your information fit into the theme, or into what others will present?

What should you try to achieve with this group? What should the audience do or not do as a result of the presentation?

By understanding demographics, shared opinions, and the event itself, you can position your information for this specific group at this specific time. To assist you, the workbook at www.FiveStepsToConquer.com has a number of worksheets to help you strategically work through these issues. Use them to enhance your presentation success.

Establish Objectives & Measure Results

It is almost impossible to overstate the value of establishing objectives for your presentations. The same applies to measuring results. Objectives and results are the precise point at which art meets science in communication. There's an old adage that you cannot improve something if you do not measure it. While it can be difficult to measure communication effectiveness, you must try to do so every time you develop and deliver a presentation. To begin the cycle of continuous improvement with your presentations, establish time-bound and measurable objectives that directly support what you and your organization are attempting to achieve.

> *Objectives should always be based on outcomes,*
> *not inputs.*

Objectives should always be based on outcomes, not inputs. In some cases, measuring results is relatively easy. Did you close the sale or get the business? Was your budget approved? Do you have support to proceed? Was a sub-committee struck? If you're delivering a persuasive presentation that encourages the audience to take fairly immediate and direct action, evaluation can boil down to answering one simple question: Did they or didn't they?

With informative presentations, measurement can be a bit trickier, especially if your objectives are weak. And when it comes to weak objectives, "raising awareness" and "informing the audience" are the weakest of all. They're the equivalent of "get the word out," or asking your children to turn the lights off in their rooms. Unless there's a benchmark of initial awareness, a study to determine concluding awareness, and results that are attributable to your presentation, "raising awareness" means nothing. It's a spray and pray approach. Spray as much information as you can and pray that some of it sticks.

Developing an effective presentation takes time and effort. There are real costs involved. Your investment—whether in your time or from your budget, or both—must bring a return. Establishing objectives and measuring results against those objectives will help you determine whether the return you get from the process is worth the investment you put in. To help you, let's take a closer look at business and communication objectives.

Business Objectives

Sometimes business objectives can be easy to quantify. Sometimes they can be elusive. Much of this can be traced to whether you're delivering a persuasive or informative presentation.

If you deliver a presentation to a management group with the intent of getting budget approval at the end of the meeting, your business success is relatively easy to quantify. Was the budget approved at the end of the meeting? Or did you have to talk to members of the management team one-on-one to get it approved? If it's the former, you achieved your objective. If it's the latter, what could you have done differently during the group presentation to get the same results you can achieve one-on-one?

It can be difficult to precisely define objectives for informative presentations.

It can be difficult to precisely define objectives for informative presentations, but you must make every attempt to do so. For example, suppose you have an idea for enhancing efficiency with a current project on which you're working, but you cannot implement this idea alone. You know this idea will be good for you, but you are unsure of its impact on others. However, you need their active buy-in to successfully implement it.

As a management group, you meet bi-weekly. You could have four or five different conversations with your counterparts prior to or after the meeting, but you decide to devote your regular update to explaining the idea and gauging their reaction to it. You contact the person organizing the meeting, and you get twenty minutes on the agenda at the end of regular updates. The updates usually go quickly because everyone submits a one-page written update at least forty-eight hours prior to the meeting, and updates at the meeting usually involve people answering questions about their submission.

Against that backdrop, your business objectives might be:

- By the end of the meeting, everyone will clearly understand how this idea could be implemented.

- By the end of the meeting, we will determine what a reasonable next step for this idea could be, and make a collective decision about whether to proceed.

Both of these objectives are time-bound and measurable. You have twenty minutes to explain the idea and facilitate a discussion about it. If people around the table don't understand the idea after twenty minutes, have you achieved your first objective? No, obviously not. For all informative presentations, create time-bound, measurable objectives for your presentations, and then measure your success in achieving those objectives within the time frame identified.

Communication Objectives

In addition to business objectives, you should establish time-bound and measurable communication objectives. All things being equal, the more you improve your communication effectiveness, the more you improve your business success, especially if the two are strongly linked from the start.

Use the following samples of communication objectives if you wish, or develop your own. When you have established your communication objectives, take a few minutes to think about how you'll determine whether you actually achieved them.

- Create a two-way exchange of information with participants that results in their asking numerous questions (i.e. at least thirty questions during a thirty-minute presentation).

- Answer participants' questions effectively during the presentation.

- Use visual aids and other tools in ways that help participants easily understand the concepts presented, but do not interfere with the message.

- Explain concepts in ways that enhance participants' understanding of them.

To determine whether you've achieved your communication objectives, it's important to formally evaluate your success. This is also where you ask yourself one important question: "What can I do to be even more successful in the future?" As you look back on your presentation, evaluate your success on the basis of two factors: your communication effectiveness and your business results.

*There are a number of signs
that can help define your success.*

When it comes to communication effectiveness, there are a number of signs that can help define your success. If the audience asks numerous questions during your presentation, that's a good sign—especially if people are applying what you say and structuring their questions around their personal circumstances. This indicates that they are relating your information to who they are as human beings, an area we'll explore more fully in *Step Five: Answer Questions Throughout.* You'll be more successful if you felt your answers were too short for you. This almost always means your answers were perfect for the audience. It leads to more questions and creates more interaction. It's more engaging.

You can also distribute a short survey or feedback sheet at the end of your presentation. There's a sample survey in the workbook. Feel free to use it directly or as a guide to help you develop your own feedback tool. If you do, you'll notice that it's strongly aligned with the five steps in this book.

Setting a benchmark and measuring communication effectiveness provides inexpensive insurance. If your presentation is not as effective as you had hoped, you can often turn to your communication objectives to determine why. From the audience's perspective, did you communicate effectively? If so, how? If not, why not? And where can you improve in the future?

Create a Strategic Approach

The deliverable product of putting the audience first is the Strategic Approach, a document that applies the models outlined in the workbook at www. FiveStepsToConquer.com and acts as a blueprint for the direction of the presentation. The document should never, ever exceed six pages in length. It should be written as prose wherever possible. Bullet points are allowed, but only if used sparingly to add identifiable value. Preferably, bullet points will be written as complete sentences.

The Strategic Approach can serve a number of purposes. It can be sent to your boss. It can be sent to the compliance department. It can be sent to co-presenters. It can be sent to conference organizers. It doesn't take long to develop. You can often obtain quick buy-in before going any further with content development. If you create these documents for your presentations, you'll improve focus and save time. Better yet, you'll clearly outline how you plan to bring their needs and your needs together.

For illustrative purposes, we're going to develop a Strategic Approach for a presentation to our local municipal council as members of the bylaw enforcement department. There's a need to implement a new barking dog bylaw in our city. The municipality has been receiving increasing numbers of resident complaints about neighborhood dogs barking between the hours of 11 p.m. and 7 a.m. The issue has escalated to the point that, at its last meeting, municipal council directed the bylaw enforcement department to conduct research and bring recommendations to the next meeting.

Nobody will complain if we don't use all thirty minutes.

As the bylaw enforcement department, we've been given thirty minutes on the agenda at council's next meeting. We're early on the agenda, because it's a full one with a controversial issue to be discussed later in the meeting. We need to be as efficient as possible. Nobody will complain if we don't use all thirty minutes.

In advance of the meeting, we're sending council an eight-page written report to be included in the agenda package. We're bringing a very short presentation for the meeting. There will be ample time for questions, whether from councilors or other attendees. Of course, councilors always have the right to ask questions at any time during staff presentations.

Need

The following needs define the initial direction of our presentation to council:

- Council members need to understand that the number of complaints has escalated significantly.

- Council members need to understand that this issue will become increasingly political if it isn't addressed soon.

- Council members need to understand that a reasonable solution is possible.

- Council needs to understand that solving this issue will promote neighborhood harmony.

Value

The value we intend to offer is:

- By the end of our presentation, council will understand that taking action now will keep a growing problem from getting out of hand.

Audience

For our barking dog presentation, we expect the mayor and all eight councilors to attend the meeting. Members of the public are generally welcome to attend meetings, but we're not aware of any person or group planning to attend this meeting to address this specific issue.

The age range of council is forty-five to seventy-five. The median age is approximately fifty-five years. The oldest is Mayor Darwish, at age seventy-five. The youngest is Councilor Higgins, at age forty-five. Half the councilors are male; half are female. The mayor is female.

The mayor has completed high school. All of the councilors have completed college or university. Two councilors have postgraduate degrees. A third holds a professional accounting designation.

Council is a very diverse group. There are two practicing Christians and two practicing Muslims. For two councilors, English is their second language. However, language will not be a barrier; all speak fluent English.

Our goal at the end of our presentation is for councilors to strike a sub-committee as the next step in the bylaw development process. They should be fairly willing to take that step. Council will be supportive of the information we're presenting. They know creating a subcommittee provides opportunities to further examine the problem and potential solutions. The subcommittee always has the option of consulting with the community, if necessary, whether formally or semi-formally.

There is an issue to be highlighted. We know that five of eight councilors are dog owners. Because they own dogs, we assume they're sympathetic to dogs, if not to their owners. If three councilors were sitting across the table from us, two of them would own dogs. That's why we're highlighting a recommendation that filing false complaints against dog owners can lead to fines.

Council members know we're following up a request they made during their last meeting. We're scheduled third at the next regular council meeting. Council members face a full agenda. The most controversial issue is a rezoning application from a developer. Many of the "smaller" items have been moved to the front of the agenda to allow for time to be spent on presentations for and against the developer's application. As staff, we are the only ones presenting on the barking dog issue.

Our goal is to outline the issue and recap the solution we provided to council in our eight-page report that was submitted in advance of the meeting. We believe a solution is possible, and our presentation will briefly outline the steps toward that solution.

Business Objectives

For this presentation, we hope to achieve two business objectives:

- Convince council to strike a subcommittee during the meeting to further investigate the issue and examine staff recommendations.

- Ensure that reporters attending the meeting understand this issue, with subsequent stories portraying it as one that can be successfully resolved.

Evaluation

After the presentation, we will evaluate our objectives in two ways. First, was a subcommittee struck? If so, we were successful. If not, we'll need to re-examine how we communicated with council and determine whether a different approach could have achieved the outcome we were seeking. Second, if there is media coverage about the issue, was it fair and accurate? How did the media position our recommendations? Did any media coverage resonate with specific communities?

Conclusion

Putting the audience first means matching what you can discuss with what they most need to hear. To be successful, you must define their need for information and translate that need into discernible value. You must understand who they are on the outside but, just as importantly, what makes them tick on the inside. It's important to gain insight into the event that brings them together. The value they receive from listening to you will shape their win.

*The Strategic Approach
helps shape your win.*

The Strategic Approach helps shape your win. What objectives would you like to accomplish? What action would you like the audience to take? How would you like them to apply your information? What business need are you satisfying?

With your strategy document in place, the next step is to develop your content. This is the subject of our next chapter, *Step Two: Structure the Conversation.*

Step Two:
Structure The Conversation

There is little doubt the promise of technology offers the opportunity to create conversations that never before existed. We have podcasts, blogs, wikis, online chats, instant messaging, e-mail, text messaging, and more. The best of each of these emulate the back-and-forth of a conversation. It's easy. Open your laptop or pick up your smart phone and type a message. Send it, and you can receive a response from someone in seconds. Over a minute, an hour, or a day, you can exchange short messages in a conversational format.

The irony of our modern world is that over the past twenty years, the form of communication that started closest to a conversation—the presentation— has been taken further and further away by technology. We would never open a text conversation with someone by typing: "I'm going to send you ten screens of information. When I've sent it, you can participate and send something back." But that's exactly what happens in modern presentations. "I'm going to go through my presentation," someone will say, "and I'll save time at the end for questions."

There are three types of presentations: Traditional, informative, and persuasive. Traditional presentations include those delivered at weddings, graduations, significant milestones, anniversaries, and funerals, to name a few. The goal is to inspire the audience to positive thoughts about the organization, the event, the person, and/or people for whom the event was organized.

*Most of us recognize that conversational
storytelling is essential.*

Most of us recognize that conversational storytelling is essential during traditional presentations. When I delivered the eulogy at my grandmother's funeral, I talked about the smell of fresh-baked bread, which was a particularly fond memory for one of my uncles. The night before the funeral, he talked about arriving home at the farm after school, and how he used to love a slice of warm buttered bread and a glass of milk before starting the evening chores. I then lightened the mood by telling everyone that my grandmother used to quietly tell me she had saved the crust for me, even though I had learned from my uncles only the evening before the funeral that none of them had ever liked the crust. She had sworn them to secrecy, a pact that they would never have broken while she was alive.

Storytelling is expected during traditional presentations. What we've forgotten, or at least what has been overshadowed by the ubiquitous use of slideware during presentations, is that storytelling is equally critical to the success of informative and persuasive presentations.

A case in the 1990s illustrates this. Three presentations were delivered to a class of MBA students who were playing the role of hard-nosed venture capitalists. Each presentation had the goal of getting funds for a startup. The first imparted the financial data. The second was a combination of financial data and story. The third simply told the story. At the end of the three presentations, the MBA students voted on which would receive funding. The successful presentation? You guessed it: The one that told the story.

The best way to inspire and persuade is through anecdotes, examples, metaphors, similes, comparisons, parables, historical events, or personal experiences—not through charts or graphs. During a video interview in 2011, a Microsoft speechwriter talks about the importance of storytelling. She exudes passion about her craft and even discusses ways in which the organization measures the success of speeches, but during the entire interview there is not even the remotest reference to PowerPoint.

People are not motivated by charts, graphs, or bullet points. They are motivated by stories told by other human beings. As that speechwriter points out during the video, audiences lean forward to listen intently to effective stories told well.

The purpose of this chapter is to define a series of models and processes by which you can develop content for your presentations, regardless of whether you're presenting to a small or large group. By applying this approach, you'll develop content that's clear, concise, and tightly focused on the needs of the specific audience in attendance. Each and every presentation you deliver will have a clear beginning, middle, and end—just like a good story.

We'll apply these models to our barking dog presentation, as an extension of the Strategic Approach from *Step One*. Using The Basic Presentation Framework, we will outline a seven-sentence story with a beginning, middle, and end. Next, we will transfer the story to a short "notes" outline that also serves as a five-minute version of our presentation. Then, we'll expand the notes outline to represent ten minutes of our portion of the conversation with council. Finally, we'll examine how to add a story to this outline to illustrate the complexity of the barking dog issue and the need for creating a new bylaw.

More Information than Time
For a number of years of my career, I worked as a freelance speechwriter. It was a fascinating training ground where I learned a number of important lessons.

There's always more information than time.

One of the most important lessons is that there's always more information than time. If people have five minutes to talk, they could probably fill ten. If they have ten, they could probably talk for twenty. If they have one hour, they could probably find enough information to fill two, especially if they are perceived as experts on the topic. But the amount of information you bring to the presentations you deliver—and, by extension, the stories you tell and the conversations you have with your audiences—is determined by the time frame you have. Period.

But if you have twenty minutes on the agenda, should you bring twenty minutes of information? No, particularly if you're planning a conversation. Bring ten. If communication truly is two-way, half the time belongs to the audience. Interactivity improves understanding, and all conversations should be interactive.

The second lesson I learned as a speechwriter is that sorting through data to match the right nuggets of information for a specific audience at that moment in time can be extremely time consuming if it's not managed properly. Early in my speechwriting career, I would enter a boardroom to tackle a new assignment, meeting from two to ten people who were there to help me. In the days before the Internet and because I may have been referred to the organization by a third party, I may not even have known what the company did when I walked into that first meeting. Chances were, however, that we would have less than two weeks to develop a finished product for either the CEO or another senior executive.

People always provided massive amounts of information to assist me. They'd provide a copy of that year's annual report, the previous year's annual report, and next year's draft. I might get articles, news releases, and other internal publications. They'd hand me copies of previous speeches. In one memorable example, the stack of information was so large that I couldn't fit it into my briefcase. Piled onto a table, it measured more than fourteen inches deep. Early in my career, I would lead a brief discussion with the group about the direction the speech should take. From there, I would take their information back to my office and write the speech.

I would work diligently to develop the best possible draft, sending it in advance or bringing it to the next meeting. I would wait breathlessly while people reviewed it. But if it happened once, it happened a hundred times. They'd read the speech, comment on the fact that it was well written, then tell me it wasn't what they would like to talk about. And we would start over.

On one project, I was hired to write a speech for a North American president of a Japanese automobile manufacturer. He wasn't involved during the initial discussions; everyone told me they knew exactly what the president wanted to say. I wrote the speech and submitted it. After the draft had been reviewed a number of times, I submitted the final speech to the client. The next day, my business partner tracked me down at another client meeting to let me know that the president wanted to call me at 4 p.m.

When we spoke on the telephone, he was very gracious about what was written (which his team had approved) but was also very clear about the fact that it wasn't what he wanted to say. He helped me understand what he wanted to accomplish. We had an excellent conversation that formed the foundation of a lasting working relationship that continued until his retirement and return to Japan. At the end of that first conversation, however, he informed me that he was catching a flight to Japan the next morning. Could I possibly fax a draft of the revised speech by 8:30 a.m. so he could review it on the flight?

The framework will sharpen your critical thinking skills.

I remember the date. It was October 31—Halloween night. My spouse and I took our children out trick-or-treating, after which I returned to the office to write the speech. At about 4:00 a.m., I realized that one of two things would have to happen. Either I would develop a better process for writing speeches, or I would find another way to make a living. And that's how The Basic Presentation Framework came into being. It's a tool that I've used countless times to write speeches, and to help my clients quickly and efficiently assemble content for their presentations. If you allow its structure and discipline to assist you, the framework will sharpen your critical thinking skills and add clarity to every presentation you deliver.

Critical Thinking and the Single Page

A close colleague is an alumnus of Procter and Gamble (P&G). She told me that one of the most important lessons she learned there was the regimen of putting ideas onto a single sheet of paper in complete sentences, not a collection of bullet points. The CEO for whom she worked demanded it. "The critical thinking skills that exercise gave me are something I've used throughout my career," she told me over one of our monthly lunches together. "The discipline of outlining a complex concept on a single page really meant the idea had to work."

A similar discipline will help you develop content for any presentation, even a one-on-one sales meeting. The Basic Presentation Framework enhances critical thinking skills by forcing you to clearly state the entire presentation from start to finish in six to eight short sentences. It doesn't matter whether you're speaking for five minutes, or conducting a five-hour continuing medical education (CME) program. The same structure applies to both challenges.

Once I started using the framework, my initial speechwriting meetings changed. I'd thank the group for the information they assembled, tell them I couldn't wait to get back to the office to read it, and then push it to one side. On a flip chart or whiteboard, I would draw a horizontal rectangular box at the top and suggest that we write down the main theme of the speech in one sentence. We'd go no further until everyone agreed to that sentence.

After completing the first sentence, I drew five horizontal rectangular boxes underneath the first. Then I informed everyone that the first two boxes represented the core of the introduction. The middle three were the main body. The last box was the conclusion.

Then I asked if everyone had heard the expression of "tell them what you're going to tell them, tell them, and tell them what you told them?" Of course, most people have heard that expression. "But," I said, "how many times have you been in the audience when it's come out as: tell them you're going to be boring, be boring and, if anyone's still awake when you get to the end, tell them you were boring?"

Bring the end to the beginning and begin there.

After a chuckle or two, we always get to a discussion of the best way to mitigate this: not to begin at the beginning, but to bring the end to the beginning and begin there. Tell the audience during your introduction what you want them to do (or not do) with the information you're presenting. Bring the call to action to the start of every presentation. This helps the audience put your information into perspective.

Those first meetings never concluded until everyone agreed to the sentences in each horizontal box. The next step was the development of an outline, similar to the notes presentation we'll develop during this chapter for our barking dog presentation. After getting reaction to the framework and outline, I made changes and resubmitted them. Once they approved the framework and outline, I returned to the mountain of information they provided to determine which specific parts actually supported the outline. We included only those that did. Everything else would be ignored, or saved for another speech to another audience.

Using this approach significantly decreased the time it took to put together content for speeches. It also changed my business model. I went from never having a speech approved at first draft to having 80 percent approved at first draft, with minimal changes or no changes at all.

Even though I no longer write speeches because I don't believe in reading scripts word for word (except in rare, extreme circumstances), I have taught this approach in workshops for twenty years. It's an excellent model for quickly and efficiently developing presentation content. Clients consistently tell me that this approach saves them countless hours in preparation.

Applying the Framework

In the top box of the framework, write the main theme of your presentation in one simple sentence, linking your objectives to the needs, wants, and desires of the audience. It should include the word "how" or "why," as in "I'd like to talk to you about how ..." or "I'd like to talk to you about why ..." Believe it or not, using one of those two words in the first sentence helps you focus on sharing information with your audience; it prevents you from downloading data.

For the barking dog presentation, the first sentence is: "We're here to talk to you about how our proposal to create a new 'barking dog' bylaw will promote neighborhood peace and harmony." Notice that the word "how" has a prominent position. This focuses your side of the conversation.

The Basic Presentation Framework

State the expected outcome
of the presentation.

Once you're satisfied with the initial sentence that captures your theme (and you shouldn't go any further until you are), the next step is to state the expected outcome of the presentation and/or the value the audience will receive. Write this down in one or two short sentences in a second narrow box under the first. As you do, remember that this box must always clearly state your call to action. In simple and straightforward terms, define the outcome you expect. You probably started developing this information when you wrote down the audience value during *Step One: Put the Audience First*.

Our barking dog presentation contains both informative and persuasive elements. On the informative side, we want members of council to understand that taking action now is important, especially if they're interested in dealing with the early stages of a growing issue. On the persuasive side, the immediate action we want them to take is to strike a subcommittee, the next step in the bylaw development process.

The first two boxes form the core of the introduction for virtually any presentation. Effective introductions capture audience attention, establish common ground between the speaker and the audience, and lead into the main body of the presentation while getting to the point as quickly as possible. The audience appreciates an interesting or creative opening, but their patience runs thin if some important questions are not answered immediately: Why should they listen? What will they get out of your presentation if they pay attention? What, precisely, should they do—or not do—as a result of the information you're presenting?

The introduction to our barking dog presentation gets to the point in three short sentences. It outlines the main theme and states the call to action. Some may call this a fairly "dry" lead, yet it establishes common ground between the speaker and audience, and immediately leads into the main body of the presentation. It gets to the point.

This raises another issue. People often wonder if they should tell a joke at the start of their presentation. The best answer is "possibly, but probably not." One of my worst nightmares as a speechwriter was working with an executive from a large bank, who probably hadn't cracked a smile in fifteen years. "Start me off with a joke," he said during our first meeting. "I'd like to be funny." Needless to say, it was a challenging project.

If you're comfortable telling jokes (and relatively good at it), and if it's appropriate, you may start with humor. However, the joke should always relate to the main theme of your presentation. Otherwise, people may later remember the joke, but not much else. And if your humor falls flat, you'll have trouble recovering your composure, which could negatively impact your presentation and your results.

These should be complete sentences, not bullet points.

The next step after your introduction is to develop the main body of your presentation: three short sentences that directly support your main theme and your call to action. These should be complete sentences, not bullet points. If you've already downloaded the workbook (from www.FiveStepsToConquer. com/workbook.html) and created a strategy document, you began developing these sentences when you defined the audience's need for information. Pick the best three or create a new set, based on the outcomes you're seeking.

Why three? Believe it or not, people tend to think in threes: yesterday, today, tomorrow; past, present, future; top, middle, bottom; left, center, right. If you have a five-step process you're explaining to a group, you might have five short sentences to briefly outline each major subject heading. Start with three, and deviate only when warranted.

Each supporting idea must be directly linked to your introduction—the main theme and the call to action that you wrote in the first two boxes at the top of the page. If an idea does not directly support your introduction, you have two choices. You can change or delete the supporting idea, or you can rework your main theme and your call to action. Your ideas should flow from start to finish. If they do not, your side of the conversation will be disjointed.

The final step is your conclusion. The conclusion is the "because" or "if" portion of your presentation. This is where you recap your main points and restate your call to action. Often, the best way to do that is through a loose syllogism or some other form of parallel structure. For example:

- Because of this ...

- Because of that ...

- And because of this third issue ...

- We hope you'll be comfortable applying the information we've discussed or taking the action we're recommending.

An effective conclusion begins
at the very start of your presentation.

An effective conclusion begins at the very start of your presentation, where you stated the call to action you expect at the end of the journey. Once you're at the destination, restate your intent. Tell them in clear and simple terms—and with all the professionalism at your disposal—how you want them to either apply your information or take action on it.

To enhance the clarity of your ideas, your entire presentation needs to be clearly and concisely stated in six to eight sentences on a single piece of paper or a single computer screen. You should be able to send this single page to a colleague, your boss, or your compliance department, and they should have a clear idea of where you're starting and where you hope to end, especially if you also include the Strategic Approach you developed in *Step One*.

Here is the Basic Presentation Framework as applied to our barking dog presentation:

> We're here to talk about how our proposal to create a new "barking dog" bylaw will promote neighborhood peace and harmony.

> By the end of our presentation, we hope you will understand that taking action now will keep a growing problem from getting out of hand. We recommend that you strike a council sub-committee tonight as the next step in the bylaw development process.

> The number of complaints we're receiving is increasing rapidly.

> We have recommended changes to the bylaw by drawing on the experience of other municipalities.

> Changing the bylaw will promote neighborhood peace and harmony.

> Because there is a rising incidence of complaints ... because other municipalities have overcome similar challenges ... and because we all believe that neighborhood harmony is important ... we are recommending that you strike a council sub-committee tonight to examine our proposal for resolving this issue.

The framework on the previous page is a broad outline of our presentation to council. It outlines the presentation from start to finish. Notice that these are sentences, not bullet points. The reason? Sentences must fit together from start to finish. The inter-relationships between ideas are clearly defined. Bullet points leave ambiguity in their wake, leading to the adage "bullet points make us stupid," which is a label neither you nor your audience wishes to wear.

Transferring the Framework: The Notes Outline

The next step is to transfer your framework to a slightly longer "notes" outline. In a pinch, this outline can serve as a three- to five-minute version of your presentation. If you only need five minutes of information for your side of the conversation, or if everyone else runs late and five minutes is all the time that's left, this is your presentation. It's your side of the conversation with the audience.

> *It's your side of the conversation*
> *with the audience.*

Notes for our barking dog presentation are on the next page. Notice that these notes are quite detailed, yet there is not a grammatically correct sentence within them. Notes are often a personal preference, but mine are for a bit more detail in my notes. The notes you use may not be this detailed (and we'll have a more detailed discussion of how to deliver notes in *Step Four: Convey Your Message and Personality*), but the important issue here is that you deliver your presentations from notes, not sentences. Use sentences to complete your framework. This ensures that your structure is sound. From there, transfer the information to notes, which is what you'll deliver your presentation from. And, quite frankly, if you wish to be more successful, do not project your notes onto a screen or hand them out in advance of your presentation.

Notes Outline—Barking Dog Presentation

- Like talk today about how proposal create barking dog bylaw --> neighborhood peace / harmony.

- By end, hope recognize action now can keep growing problem getting out of hand.
    ◦ Recommend strike subcommittee 2nite / next step process.

- Cover following points:
    ◦ Number barking dog complaints increasing rapidly.
    ◦ Recommended changes draw on benchmarks / experience other municipalities.
    ◦ Changes promote neighborhood peace / harmony.

- Number barking dog complaints increasing rapidly.
    ◦ Fewer than 20 complaints per year 2000 — dogs barking 11 pm – 7 am.
    ◦ This year 20 complaints / month.
    ◦ No question growing problem / growing awareness of problem.

- Recommended changes draw on benchmarks / experience other municipalities.
    ◦ All cases, complaint lodged by neighbor followed up.
    ◦ Complaint valid? — dog owner given warning.
    ◦ Complaints continue? — fines begin $50 / escalate from there.
    ◦ Filing false complaint? — first warning then $50 fine.

- Changes promote neighborhood peace / harmony.
    ◦ Reasonable expect no constant barking overnight.
    ◦ Experience other municipalities show less enforcement needed over time.
    ◦ Experience other municipalities shows allows neighbors focus being neighbors.

Conclusion

- Because number complaints increasing rapidly ...

- Because other municipalities overcome similar challenges ...

- Because neighborhood harmony important ...

- We hope you endorse recommendations: strike subcommittee review proposal / implement solution.
  - ° Goal keep growing problem getting out of hand.

Winston Churchill, perhaps one of the greatest orators of the 20th century, was quoted as saying that a speaker should spend one hour per finished minute preparing a speech. Sir Winston believed that if the speech is twenty minutes long, the speaker should spend at least twenty hours preparing it. Has technology improved our productivity? No, it has not. Today, the suggestion is that a speaker should spend up to ninety hours developing a sixty-minute presentation with PowerPoint support, with at least one-third of that time spent preparing the slides.[vi]

Who has that kind of time to develop a presentation?

Who has that kind of time to develop a presentation? If you're preparing a presentation for a road show that you're going to deliver dozens of times to launch a new product or service, such an investment may be worth the effort. You're going to amortize it over a series of presentations. But if you're preparing a one-time presentation to a board of directors, a senior management team, or a municipal council, can you afford to spend two full weeks preparing it? Possibly, but probably not.

If you believe that conversations are important to engagement, your goal should be to create a two-way exchange with the audience in which up to half the allotted time belongs to them. By following this logic, and applying The Basic Presentation Framework to build your content from the ground up, you will reduce your preparation time.

Expanding Your Content

If you need more than five minutes for your side of the conversation, your next step is to expand your notes outline. By adhering to this systematic process, you're building your information from the ground up, making it easier to adhere to the principle of "less is more."

This is exactly opposite from what happens when content is developed on a program like PowerPoint or Keynote. When you start with slideware, the tendency is to assemble too much information. By the time you gather it all, you fall in love with every piece. Typing your content into bullet points on slides and adding charts and graphs makes each individual piece of information more difficult to remove because, as crazy as it sounds, we actually develop emotional attachments to information.

During the editing process for a speech on which I was working nearly twenty-five years ago, I watched somewhat amused as two managers engaged in a heated discussion about why their specific information should be included in the vice-president's speech. In the end, he included none of the disputed content.

I was less amused when the executive suggested we take out half a dozen consecutive paragraphs from the speech. I thought they were the best paragraphs I had written in a long time. He agreed, but then told me to read that section of the speech twice, once with the paragraphs in and once without them. "If the meaning doesn't change when you take them out," he said, "leave them out." I'll be darned if he wasn't right. It's a guideline I've tried to remember for past twenty-five years.

Expanding the notes outline for our barking dog presentation is relatively easy, but still requires discipline. In the original notes outline, we had three points supporting our main theme. From there, we added three ideas to support each point. To expand this outline, we're going to keep our original three points, but increase the amount of information under each.

This is done in the following example, in which the barking dog presentation has been expanded to about ten minutes of information. This leaves us plenty of time within our thirty-minute time slot on the council's agenda, especially considering we already sent them an eight-page report in advance of the meeting. With this content, we still have enough time to strategically insert a story into the presentation that highlights the necessity of developing a new bylaw.

Expanded Notes: "Barking Dog" Presentation

- Like talk today about how proposal create barking dog bylaw --> neighborhood peace / harmony.

- By end, hope recognize action now keep growing problem getting out of hand.
    - Recommend strike subcommittee 2nite next step process.

- Cover following points:
    - Number barking dog complaints increasing rapidly.
    - Recommended changes draw on benchmarks / experience other municipalities.
    - Changes promote neighborhood peace / harmony.

- Number barking dog complaints increasing rapidly recent years.
    - In 2000, received less than 20 complaints per year dogs barking 11 pm-7 am.
    - First year ever kept records.
    - Issue hit city's "radar" — became aware really was issue.
    - This year received 20 complaints / month.
    - More than ten-fold increase last decade.
    - Issue going from small blip to large one — community radar.
    - No question growing problem / growing awareness of problem.
    - People not only looking at issue themselves / talking to neighbors & friends.
    - Complaints isolated to specific neighborhoods but growing — both # neighborhood & # complaints each neighborhood.

- Recommended changes draw on benchmarks / experience other municipalities.
  - All cases, complaint lodged by neighbor followed up.
  - Visit by bylaw officer / goal 24 hrs.
  - Discuss complaint both neighbors / try negotiate resolution.
  - Complaint valid? — dog owner given warning.
  - Emphasis on education this stage / get neighbors talking each other.
  - Fines used last resort / cannot get resolution early stages.
  - Complaints continue? — fines begin $50 / escalate from there.
  - Fines increase as number visits continue / maximum $500.
  - Filing false complaint? — first warning then $50 fine.

- Changes promote neighborhood peace / harmony.
  - Reasonable no constant barking overnight.
  - Consistent municipality's existing noise bylaw.
  - Neighbors have right to quiet / overnight hours.
  - Experience other municipalities --> less enforcement over time.
  - Works well — get neighbors talking each other.
  - Underscores importance negotiating / educating neighbors.
  - Experience other municipalities —> neighbors focus being neighbors.
  - Best outcomes neighbors talking each other / helping solve local issues.
  - Numerous examples of neighbors actually becoming closer after bylaw enforcement visit.

Conclusion

- Because number complaints increasing rapidly ...

- Because other municipalities overcome similar challenges ...

- Because neighborhood harmony important ...

- We hope you endorse recommendations: strike subcommittee review recommendations / implement solution.
  - ° Goal keep growing problem from getting out of hand.

Not every presentation is less than twenty minutes in length.

Yes, I know what you're thinking. Not every presentation is less than twenty minutes in length. True, but the world would be a better place if more were.

We felt we didn't need more than ten minutes of information, since we sent an eight-page document to council in advance of the meeting. The document was organized along three topic areas that parallel our oral presentation. However, the document was printed in a vertical format, because our director of bylaw enforcement correctly believes that documents printed in vertical (portrait) formats have enhanced readability over those printed in horizontal (landscape) formats. We also believe that it's the responsibility of council members to read written information in advance of the meeting, which is why we aren't planning to walk them through the document.

With longer presentations, your introduction will be similar to what you prepared for your five-minute notes outline. You may also have time to use a creative opening with a longer time frame. Also, longer presentations sometimes mean dealing with housekeeping items. You may have to introduce yourself or other presenters. There may be people to thank. The housekeeping items you deal with and the creative tools you use will depend on the circumstances, audience, objectives, and time frame for each specific presentation, most of which you'll identify by working through *Step One* and creating your Strategic Approach document.

Completing Your Content

Once you've expanded your notes outline or your framework, the final step is to selectively insert analogies, comparisons, stories, case studies, group exercises, anecdotes, statistics, and other tools to help bring your presentation to life and make it relevant to participants. You'll notice that visual aids appear nowhere on this list. This is because your content needs to be complete before a single visual aid is conceived or created. If we want to reduce 'Death by PowerPoint,' we need to create visual aids *last*, not *first*, in the content-development process.

There are a variety of narrative tools to help you.

Theoretically, there are a variety of narrative tools to help you achieve your communication outcomes. For our barking dog presentation, we believe a single story helps put the issue—and the need for new legislation—into perspective for council:

"When we conducted research to determine how other municipalities have dealt with similar issues, we discovered that one of the most important steps is to follow up within twenty-four hours. The goal is to have bylaw enforcement officers open dialogue between dog owners and anyone who files complaints. As a result of the research, the bylaw enforcement department immediately implemented twenty-four hour response, and one specific situation illustrated the need for an enhanced bylaw.

"The case involved a homeowner who let her dog out into her backyard before her shower each morning at 6:00 a.m. The dog is a small terrier, a nice enough animal except that it barks at the slightest provocation. Even a gust of wind will set it off. Neighbors who like to sleep with their windows open were constantly awakened at 6:00 a.m. Records indicated that a number of neighbors had complained in the past, but they had been told there was little that could be done. The noise bylaw was designed to deal with loud parties, not barking dogs.

"After receiving another complaint, the bylaw enforcement officer visited the homeowner, who admitted to knowing that her dog barked, but had never been approached by her neighbors about the issue. When she learned that it was disturbing them, she said: 'I just assumed they'd shut their windows if it bothered them.' When the homeowner was made aware that her neighbors were disturbed, she agreed to alter her morning schedule.

"This illustrates the need for a new bylaw to supplement the processes we've already put in place. This homeowner was reasonable, but she could just as easily have said that her morning schedule was her morning schedule, and if her neighbors didn't like the barking, they could sleep with their windows closed. If she did say those words, our hands would be tied. The current bylaw does not allow us to impose reasonable solutions or penalties."

This story would be inserted into the second section of the presentation to council, but not included in the written report. The story will be told, not read, during the meeting. The director of bylaw enforcement believes that this story illustrates the need for a new bylaw and will help motivate council to take the action we're recommending.

This enables them to remember your ideas.

There are a variety of narrative tools that can be used to bring life to your presentations—to engage your audiences in ways that capture their imagination and make it possible for them to effectively integrate working and long-term memory. Tools like asking rhetorical questions, using quotes from recognized personalities, creating comparisons, introducing provocative concepts, and making promises—a list that is by no means exhaustive—help audience members find a place for your information within their existing cognitive framework. This enables them to remember your ideas long after you've left the room.

There are a host of tools, which are limited only by your creativity and whether each tool is appropriate for helping you reach your objectives. But the bottom line is simple. Every tool you use and every story you tell must support your strategic objectives. Period.

Framework: A Time-Saving, Flexible Tool

I recently read a blog article on the Internet that espouses creating a presentation in four hours. The first fifteen minutes is spent defining objectives, including an analysis of the audience. The next forty-five minutes is spent out-lining content and visualizing how you'll actually conduct your presentation. The remaining three hours is spent developing slides.[vii]

It's easy to identify the origin of 'Death by PowerPoint' when less than one-sixteenth of preparation time is spent thinking about the audience and 75 percent is spent messing about with slides. Those time frames should be reversed. Three hours should be spent analyzing the audience, defining objec-tives, and developing content. Actually, when you become comfortable with the models in *Step One* and *Step Two*, particularly as they are outlined in the workbook at FiveStepsToConquer.com, you'll discover that you probably won't need all three hours. And if you use milestones for your visuals (that we'll soon cover in *Step Three*), you won't need even an hour to complete your slides.

The Basic Presentation Framework is an extremely useful and flexible tool that can be applied to every presentation challenge you face. It helps clarify your thinking, enables you to focus on the needs of the audience, and assists you with adhering to the principle of "less is more." I can't count the number of times that people have told me that they continue to use this tool five, ten, fifteen, or more years after they've attended one of my workshops.

The framework can be used to develop a presentation of any length.

The framework can be used to develop presentations of any length. And its premise is simple. If you can't clearly define your side of the conversation in six to eight sentences, don't expect a sixty-minute time frame to rescue you. If your ideas are not clear in the shorter format, they'll never be clear in the longer one.

Step Three:
Minimize Visual Aids

In 1981, during my last year of college, I worked a field placement at a corporation that happened to be preparing a series of employee meetings, the presentations for which were delivered by members of the senior management team. The meetings were scheduled for a number of geographic locations. Each executive delivered a number of presentations, depending on their geographic region or business line. The year I arrived was the first in which senior executives used 35-mm slides to support their talks.

I spent hours putting slides upside-down into carousels, double-checking each carousel to ensure that all were in proper order and identical to each other. At the time, each slide cost seventy-five dollars to produce. There were six carousels, each with about thirty slides. The total cost was about $14,000—a significant sum even by today's standards. More than thirty years ago, with the Dow Jones Industrial Average languishing below a thousand points, it was a staggering amount to spend. If you asked the people who produced these slides and profited from them if slides were necessary, what would they say? Of course! Your executives want to look professional, don't they?

Today, given the change in the value of a dollar, those same slides would cost $250 each to produce. I've often thought that this would be an excellent way to encourage people to minimize the visuals they use. Imagine that your first five slides were "free" but you had to donate $250 to your favorite charity for every additional slide you print or project. Even if the charitable organization was the best on the planet, chances are your thirty-slide presentations would be whittled down to three or four in no time, and 'Death by PowerPoint' would become a fleeting memory.

It means questioning the value
of each and every slide.

Minimizing visual aids means questioning the value of each and every slide you use—whether you project it, print it, or both. Adding a slide because the image on the screen hasn't changed for a while is not a valid reason for creating another visual and will not help minimize the number you use.

Some people set the timing for their presentation by counting the number of slides they use (i.e. one slide for every minute of the presentation). For a sixty-minute time frame, even if the presenter believes half the time belongs to the audience, he or she is still bringing thirty slides. This may be appropriate, but only if each and every slide is examined and the answer to "Is this slide really necessary?" is "Yes!".

Likewise, it's unrealistic to dictate an arbitrary number of slides per presentation. I provided one-on-one presentation coaching to a senior executive who told me he'd attended a presentation skills program that recommended ten slides per presentation. "What if you only need none or only one?" I asked. "Are you supposed to come up with nine or ten more? What about instances in which you legitimately need more than ten?"

He just shrugged his shoulders. Apparently, he and others had asked those questions during the workshop, but never really received an answer. I suspect this advice emanates from Guy Kawasaki's 10/20/30 suggestion. Mr. Kawasaki is a venture capitalist who sits through presentations from inventors and would-be entrepreneurs. In his worldview, when you're asking him for money, you should never bring more than ten slides per presentation. Your presentation should never exceed twenty minutes. And you should never use a font size less than thirty-point.

Fair enough. These are his guidelines, and as the receiver of ideas for which he might provide capital, he has every right to apply 10/20/30. What's most interesting about his perspective, however, is that he specifically refers to one-hour time frames in which these presentations are delivered. He believes the presentation should take no more than twenty minutes, leaving two-thirds of the available time (forty minutes) for the conversation. Smart presenters would structure a conversation from the beginning, thereby devoting the entire hour to a back-and-forth exchange. If the underlying idea is even remotely valuable, this is the best way to convince Mr. Kawasaki to part with his capital.

> *Your visual aids should supplement your story,*
> *not the other way around.*

We should only use visual aids when there is absolutely no other alternative to effectively explaining our ideas. During a lunch conversation, if you feel the need to use a napkin to draw a picture that will help the other person understand, that may be a good place to use some form of visual during a group presentation. However, when we get to the larger presentation, it's not enough to simply flash a completed graph, chart, or diagram at the audience and expect them to immediately understand its meaning. We should draw the picture for the group the same way we did one-on-one over lunch, whether freehand or digitally. In other words, whether we're using a whiteboard, a flip chart, a blackboard, or a whiteboard program on our smartphone or tablet—or whether we're using PowerPoint or Keynote—we should build the diagram at the same rate and in the same sequence as we drew it on the napkin.

Your visual aids should supplement your story, not the other way around. When you need visuals, use visuals. When they no longer serve a purpose, remove them from audience view. In a pinch, this can easily be accomplished by pushing the *b* or *w* key on the keyboard of the computer from which the slides are projected. The *b* key turns the screen black. The *w* key turns the screen white.

Testing the Assumption of Success

For more than a decade, I've questioned the validity of using too many slides during presentations. Actually, I have often questioned the validity of using slides at all, especially in situations where they seemed unnecessary to the challenge of communicating effectively to achieve business results.

In 2003, after my presentation to a group of financial services professionals on the west coast, one of the participants, a very successful financial advisor, approached me and said: "I was fascinated by the part of your presentation where you talked about slides getting in the way of the communication process. My business partner and I proved that to ourselves without a doubt."

He told me that he and his partner have built a significant portion of their business through financial seminars to clients and prospects. At the time we spoke, they had delivered presentations and/or seminars once or twice a week for years, and had the process down to a science.

They kept their seminar topics current and presented the information themselves. They carefully selected and segmented their prospects. They knew how many people their marketing assistants needed to contact to fill a seminar (always kept to fewer than twenty participants). Based on attendance, they knew how many subsequent meetings they should book and how many new accounts they should open as a result of every seminar conducted.

This worked well until the partner had an idea. "In the late 1990s, my partner said that, if we wanted to have a modern, professional presentation that people would take seriously, we should use overheads," the advisor said. "I agreed to go along, but a number of conditions had to be met."

The first was that they would take time to carefully prepare their presentation. Next, they would practice until they were very comfortable before delivering their presentation to prospects. Finally, they would deliver the same presentation for an eight-week period, after which they would measure the results.

They carefully prepared the presentation, rehearsed it, and delivered it once or twice a week for the eight-week period. They were surprised when they measured their outcomes.

Bookings for face-to-face meetings dropped by 25 percent.

"Based on the number of people attending, bookings for face-to-face meetings dropped by 25 percent during the eight weeks in question," he said.

"As soon as we went back to the 'old' way of telling stories and drawing pictures on flip charts, our numbers went back up."

The numbers stayed up until his partner had another idea. He said that everyone was now using PowerPoint and that, to be taken seriously, they needed to change the way they delivered their seminars.

The same conditions were imposed, but this time they practiced their presentation even more before unleashing it on prospects. "In the eight-week period during which we used PowerPoint, our bookings for follow-up meetings with prospects dropped by 50 percent," the advisor told me. "Again, when we went back to a simple approach, those numbers went back up and have stayed up ever since."

Is this investment advisor on the right track? Yes, for a couple of reasons. First, he and his partner are closing the communication loop. They're focused on outcomes, not inputs. Telling people is not enough. Sending your message is not enough. What matters is whether people are applying what you're telling them or taking action on it. In this case, the action was to book a follow-up meeting. Effective communicators focus on the outcomes they seek from every presentation they deliver, regardless of whether it's informative or persuasive.

For example, let's suppose you're a researcher in health care who delivers presentations to doctors, nurses, and other clinicians on how they can provide information to assist your research. To close the communication loop after your presentations, you must determine if they're giving you the information you need. If so, perfect! If not—or if you only get usable information 70 percent of the time—what can you do to improve your results? If you're using slides to deliver your information, perhaps you should use other tools to get the outcomes you're seeking. Change your inputs to enhance your outcomes. Don't settle with simply conveying your message. That's never good enough.

There is virtually no direct evidence to indicate
that slide-driven presentations are effective.

This investment advisor is on the right track for another reason: he's questioning the efficacy of slide-driven presentations. He should. As we discussed before, there is virtually no direct evidence to indicate that slide-driven presentations are effective.

Separate Spoken from Written

A couple of important principles about using visual aids underscore the importance of separating spoken and written language (orality and literacy) to communicate effectively. The first is that human beings cannot read and listen at the same time. This is actually quite easy to prove.

The next time you're watching your favorite all-news channel, try listening to the announcer while reading what's scrolling across the bottom. Even if both oral and written information are related to the same story, it shouldn't take longer than ten or fifteen seconds to figure out that if you want to get anything of value from what's coming from the television, you either have to: a. read and block out what the announcer is saying, or b. listen to the announcer and ignore the written information. By trying to do both, you overload working memory and get less than if you do either one separately.

The second principle of visual aids is that if people have a choice between receiving information through their eyes or their ears, they tend to pick their eyes. Put up a slide, flip the page in the deck, or put an investment plan in front of a client, and their eyes immediately turn to the visual. However, once their eyes go there, it becomes increasingly difficult for them to listen to what you're saying.

> *The spoken and written word
> should always be separate.*

Orality and literacy—the spoken word and the written word—should always be separate, regardless of whether you're delivering a presentation to a thousand people or speaking with someone one-on-one. Investment advisors who walk clients through investment plans are kidding themselves. Clients will look at the plan and start reading, completely blocking what the investment advisor is saying in order to get anything out of reading the plan. Alternatively, they must lift their head and ignore the plan if they wish to get anything from what their advisor is saying. If they try to do both, the research is clear: They get less than if they focus on either one separately.

But they cannot stop themselves from reading. And because they don't want to be rude, they try to keep one ear tuned to their advisor while they read about how their wealth and dreams have been translated into dollars, pounds, euros, or yen. As a result, they retain nothing, leading investment advisors to lament that "clients never understand us." With the use of bullet points—any bullet points—as well as charts, graphs, and infographics, the same process occurs on a daily basis during group presentations the world over. People are trying to read, think, and listen at the same time. As a result, they retain little, if anything at all.

The investment plan, like all comprehensive handouts, should be either sent in advance of the meeting, or provided at the end to reinforce what was discussed. Decisions on whether to provide handouts at the beginning or end are influenced by a number of factors, including audience preference. The conversation should be structured, but held in isolation from the written document. Pictures can be drawn when necessary on a whiteboard, flip chart, or piece of paper strategically positioned between the advisor and the client. If a predeveloped graph, chart, or other image is needed, keep it from audience view until the appropriate moment.

Explain the image before it's shown. What's the relationship between the X and Y axis? Why is this important? How does it impact the portfolio? When the chart or graph is revealed, stop talking until the client absorbs its meaning. Start talking again only after the client has lifted his or her head and is ready to listen. Human beings can't think and listen at the same time. They can't read and listen at the same time. And they definitely can't think, read, and listen at the same time. The sender of information needs to recognize this and stop talking when the receiver is thinking. When people lift their head from the document, ideally the first words out of the sender's mouth should be: "Are there any questions?" Once the visual is no longer needed, remove it from view.

Apply a similar process
to group presentations.

To enhance effectiveness, apply a similar process to group presentations. If you plan to use a relatively complex visual, explain to the audience in advance what they're about to see and why it's important. Whether you're projecting a slide, handing out a spreadsheet with dozens of cells, or referring to an income statement in the package you sent in advance, the same process applies. Tell them the relevance of what they're about to see and then turn their attention to it. Once you do, let them absorb its meaning in silence. Stop talking until they're once again ready to listen.

When they bring their attention back to you, ask if there are any questions. Then pause again. Don't go through your explanation a second time, unless someone specifically asks for it. Answer all questions, and then remove the visual from the field of view.

If you're putting a case study on-screen to facilitate discussion, show the case study but don't read it to the audience. Let them read it to themselves in silence. When you no longer need it, remove it from view. Blank the screen by pushing the *b* or *w* key on your keyboard, or insert another milestone.

If a handout has been sent, assume the audience has read it.

If a handout has been sent in advance, assume the audience has read it. Do not "present it" or "walk them through it" when everyone gets together. If needed, your presentation should be an overview recapping the main points, as we did with our barking dog presentation. Answer questions and move on.

The exchange of ideas is the true value of bringing people together face-to-face, whether in person or through some form of technology, like a video call or a teleseminar. When people can talk to each other, understanding is created through meaningful dialogue and discussion. As we'll explore during the next two chapters, you need to deliver your ideas conversationally and—wherever even remotely and physically possible—answer questions throughout.

A Range of Tools

We are at a point where people automatically equate "slide" with "visual aid." In fact, if you tell someone you're using a visual aid for your presentation, what are the chances they'll automatically think of a PowerPoint or Keynote slide? Probably very high. But this connection is too limiting. We have a range of tools at our disposal. The appropriate tool needs to be selected and applied to the challenge of communicating effectively.

In an interesting YouTube video, for example, a consultant uses a lemon to explain successful negotiation. "Seems pretty simple," he says. "I have two parties, party A and party B. Both want the lemon." He cuts the lemon. "I give the two parties to this dispute 50 percent of the available resources. You'd think they would be happy."

But they are not happy. They cannot achieve 50 percent of their goals. In fact, when he probes, he discovers neither can achieve anything.

However, by listening to their concerns, he realizes that one party wants to make lemonade and needs the juice from the lemon. "That's pretty easy," he explains, reaching for another prop. "I've got a juicer and that party can be satisfied."

He discovers that the other party wants to make a cake with lemon frosting and only needs the rind. He picks up a peeler. "By peeling the lemon, (one) party can be 100 percent satisfied," he concludes. "And by juicing the lemon, (the other) party can be 100 percent satisfied—when there was no satisfaction before."[viii]

> ### *This exact process helped make Steve Jobs the admired communicator.*

Is this consultant using a visual aid? Of course he is. And he can deliver exactly the same presentation whether he is talking to one person or ten thousand. In fact, as a true test of communication effectiveness, he could convey these ideas over the telephone without any props. However, if he was delivering the presentation to a large room of ten thousand people, what would be the visual? Instead of PowerPoint, the audio-visual company could use a video camera to capture a medium shot of him using his props that would be projected onto the screen. That way, everyone in the room would have an unobstructed view of his demonstration. It's this exact process that helped make Steve Jobs the admired communicator he became.

Marshall McLuhan introduced us to "the medium is the message." The idea is that the form of communication someone uses shapes how the message is communicated and perceived. Depending on whether a perception needs to be created, reinforced, or changed, as well as the audience's characteristics and need for information, we have a variety of tools to help us inform or influence others. They range from a knife, a juicer, and a lemon to flip charts, whiteboards, and a blank piece of paper between salesperson and client, to printed income statements, balance sheets, and spreadsheets with dozens of cells filled with numbers that can be handed to the audience when needed. Slides are somewhere in between, but they are not the only tool to help us communicate effectively.

Imagine that the mechanic where you get your vehicle serviced has only one tool to complete the job. Can he or she successfully fix your vehicle with only a screwdriver or crescent wrench? Possibly, but probably not. By the same token, if slides are the only communication tool you use, you are limiting your potential for success. Certainly, there may be times when you'll be successful. But there will be many more times when you'll be less successful. If you limit the size of your toolbox, be prepared to limit your results.

I recently enrolled in an introductory French course at a local college. One evening per week, from 6:30 to 9:30 p.m., I have been immersed in a stimulating learning environment in which the instructor uses a wide range of visual aids to facilitate the transfer of her information to us.

She uses whiteboards and chalkboards to help explain rules of grammar. She even uses (gasp!) an overhead projector to show detailed charts of regular adjectives in their masculine, feminine, singular, and plural forms. Are overhead acetates different from PowerPoint slides? Yes. You can get much more readable information onto an acetate than a slide, and you can write on the acetate. Ergo, it's another tool to be considered and implemented. She uses various forms of flash cards, and a host of visual tools to help her communicate language concepts. And she's extremely effective. Interestingly, the one tool she doesn't use is PowerPoint, even though our classroom, like most college classrooms today, has an LCD projector mounted on the ceiling and a computer chained to the front of the room.

Professor McLuhan did not leave us with "the medium dictates the message." However, with the overuse of slideware, that's the point to which modern presentations have evolved. "Do you have a deck?" someone will ask. "I presented the deck to the clients," someone else will say. "Can you send your slides in advance of the meeting?" is another question we've all heard. If you need to send information in advance, send it. But don't present the same deck or document when you get together.

Is this visual aid absolutely necessary?

For every slide or visual aid you use in any presentation, ask yourself two questions.

- Is this visual aid absolutely necessary?
- Will this visual aid interfere with the conversation?

The answers to these questions must be "yes" and "no," respectively. Yes, the visual is absolutely necessary. No, it doesn't interfere with the conversation. Only then should you include it. If the visual isn't absolutely necessary, or if it will interfere with the conversation in any way, don't use it. Blank the screen and talk to your audience.

Using Milestones

If you feel compelled to project something in front of the audience at all times, using "milestone" slides is an excellent approach that solves the dilemma of too many slides or no slides at all. It also provides an excellent framework for handouts. To illustrate this, let's turn our attention back to our barking dog presentation.

For our presentation to council, we have decided to use PowerPoint. Our approach, however, is to use milestones as visuals and include one graph. The decision to include the graph caused some internal debate. Some people believed it wasn't necessary. When you tell people that complaints increased from twenty per year to twenty per month over a period of ten years, they are intelligent enough to draw their own picture. However, in the end, the graph was included.

The director will use notes to stay on track and on time while delivering her presentation, but none of her notes will be projected onto the screen. The visuals will simply be broad subject headings as a way to keep people focused on the three sections of her presentation.

With this in mind, her visuals will be:

The Need for a New
'Barking Dog' Bylaw

Mary Beth Struthers
Director, Bylaw Enforcement

Complaints
Increasing Rapidly

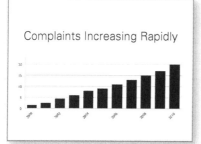

Recommended
Changes

Neighbourhood
Peace & Harmony

The maximum number of words per slide is four.

These are milestones. Except for the title slide (which contains fourteen words), the maximum number of words per slide is four. There's one graph. Each slide is a broad subject heading that simply outlines major sections of the presentation.

If you're driving from Philadelphia to New York, you don't pass a sign that says: "If you maintain an average speed of seventy miles per hour, you should reach New York in approximately 1.186 hours." The sign simply says: "New York 83." The remaining information is filled in with your own insight or through a conversation with a passenger, neither of which is likely to encompass three decimal points like the exact calculation above.

I have used this milestone tactic extensively over the past few years. I often present the ten principles of effective communication we'll examine in the next chapter during conferences and meetings under the title "Present With Ease." For years, I refused to use PowerPoint or Keynote during these presentations. I used a whiteboard or flip chart, or a chalkboard if that's all that was available. In many cases, I used nothing at all.

At least 90 percent of the time, people didn't even notice a lack of slides. In fact, at one presentation, someone asked me how I could think it possible to deliver a professional presentation without using slides. I didn't know what to say, since I hadn't used a single slide during the previous forty-five minutes. As I was thinking of a response, people started giggling, which soon led to outright laughter. When she realized what she had just said, she added: "I'm not talking about you, I'm talking about the rest of us looking professional."

Over the years, however, people have often come up after my presentations and asked how they could possibly reconcile my approach with the reality of their organization. They felt that PowerPoint was expected in their organization, and they could not consider delivering a presentation without having something projected onto the screen at all times.

A few years ago, I relented and began using milestones for my "Present With Ease" conference presentation. Depending on the environment, I would project slides onto the screen, or print them out as three-per-page handouts and use that as the guide for my presentation. I have done both with excellent results.

The slides for this sixty- to ninety-minute presentation are below (reading from left to right across each row of slides):

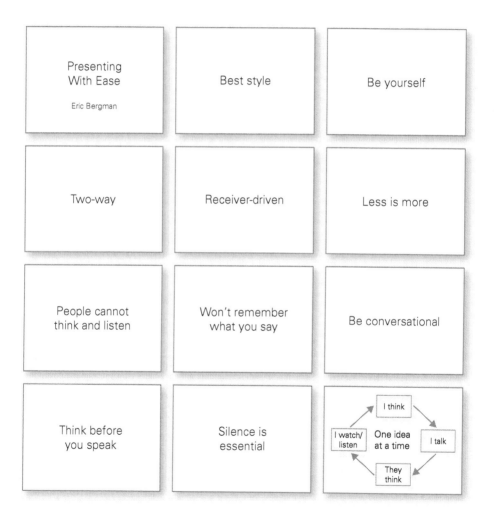

The milestone format works well with handouts provided during a presentation and are something we'll discuss a bit later. But let's now turn our attention to the diagram from the slides above. This slide is projected onto the screen but not included in the handout. The assumption is made (and has been borne out over hundreds of presentations) that people will draw the diagram on their notes handout as it is revealed on-screen. In other words, by leaving this diagram out of the handout, the goal is to encourage greater participation by having people actually draw it themselves when it's revealed. The trick, however, is to build the diagram electronically the same way it's drawn on a flip chart or whiteboard.

Prior to ever including this diagram on a Keynote slide, I had drawn it freehand thousands of times on whiteboards and flip charts for a host of audiences. The following script provides an idea of how this diagram has been revealed, one step at a time, to audiences when Keynote is used.

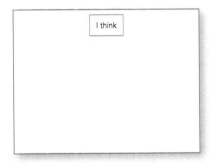

"There's a pattern that forms in good conversations and, by extension, effective presentations. The pattern begins with 'I think.' Not only is thinking before talking a good thing, this pattern emulates the way we've talked about using notes. Glance down quickly to get your next note, then look up and think, in silence. Turn that one note into a full idea, which represents no more than about twenty words of talking.

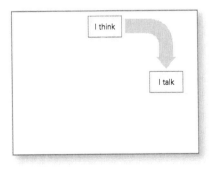

"Once you've taken a second or two to think about what you're going to say, the next step is 'I talk.' You're now going to express that idea as quickly as you can. Remember, there are two components of pace: Rate of word delivery and rate of ideas. Whether you're talking to one person or a thousand, you want to get the words out quickly if you're enthusiastic about the concepts you're discussing. But you need to pause between ideas to give the audience an opportunity to absorb what you've said.

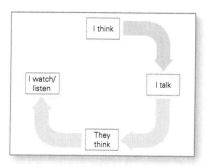

"Once you've expressed your idea, whose turn is it to think now? It's the audience's turn. The pause for them to think is critical. One of the principles we've already discussed is that human beings will not remember what you say. They will remember what they thought about what you've said. If you don't give them time to absorb your ideas—to relate what you've said to who they are as individuals—they won't remember much of anything. 'They think' is therefore vital.

"While they're thinking, what do you do? You watch and listen. This is where you look for the nods and 'uh-huhs' that signal they've processed one idea and are ready for the next. Of course, if you see a puzzled expression, should you keep talking? No. Stop and ask: "Are there any questions?"

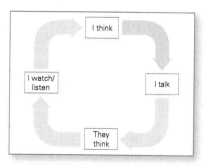

"Once you've received the signal that people are ready for more, you start the process again by glancing at your next note, lifting your head, and thinking again. This pattern happens one idea at a time in good conversations and effective presentations.

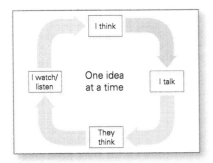

"There are two types of silence. One is for you to think; as we've discussed, thinking before talking is a good thing. The other is for *them* to think. If they do not take time to think about your ideas, they will internalize and retain very little and your communication effectiveness will suffer."

As the diagram is revealed, it's important to pause extensively. Anyone who has ever been inside a classroom knows that you cannot write and listen at the same time. As people are writing down the next step in the diagram, it's important to allow them to do so. Stop talking. As they start coming back, continue with your next idea.

The more complex the diagram, the longer it should take to impart it to the audience. I once worked with a client to redevelop a presentation that was part of a road show she was delivering. She was not getting the results she was seeking, so she contacted me to see if I could help.

After viewing her original presentation and going through the process of defining need, value, audience, and objectives, it became apparent that one of the diagrams she was flashing to prospects was critical to the success of her presentation. Once they understood the diagram, the rest of the logic of what she was saying simply fell into place.

We broke the diagram into smaller pieces and two-thirds of her presentation was devoted to unfolding that diagram one piece at a time. Her results immediately improved.

Using Pictures

There's a line of thinking that believes pictures, instead of bullet points, should be used as slides. The intent of this advice is certainly good. We all know bullet points are at the core of 'Death by PowerPoint' because they are a sign that the presentation's content has been developed from the slideware program. However, the drawback to switching to pictures is that the entire presentation can become a march through a series of pictures. While this will be visually stimulating for the audience, they'll miss large portions of what the presenter is saying while they're examining picture after picture. Using pictures seems to be much more effective when the audience is given an idea in advance of what to look for.

To explain this, let's suppose I'm an architect, and your firm has hired me to design a new building. The facility will house your corporate offices and include a large warehouse as a major shipping hub. A number of your senior executives provided insight into their requirements as part of the development process.

The vice-president of human resources said that one of his primary wishes was to have a bright and cheerful reception area. "It's the first thing our customers, suppliers, and other visitors see," he said. "I want the reception area to make a positive first impression on everyone who comes here." During the meeting, I make careful note of his wishes.

The vice-president of product and service development says that her biggest concern is creating an environment conducive to teamwork. The work space for her group must be extremely flexible. There may be situations in which teams need to be assembled on a moment's notice. Other times, groups may work together for weeks. I make note of her ideas.

The vice-president of distribution has still different concerns. "The doors on our current loading dock are too narrow," he said during one of our meetings. "It's difficult to get product in and out. A bright reception area is nice and work space is important, but I need wider doors. As we grow, moving product in and out will become even more critical."

What should I use as a visual aid?

I make note of these thoughts and more, then go back to my office to design a new building. Once my design is complete, I now have some choices to make for my presentation to the senior management team. One of these is: What should I use as a visual aid? I decide to construct a scale model of the building, which I then present.

I begin by saying that I have positioned the building on the footprint of the land and faced it southwest. I built the reception area out from the main building and enclosed it in glass—UV protective glass, so the receptionist and visitors will not require sunscreen. However, if there is even a hint of sunshine, the reception area will be the warmest and friendliest in the entire industrial park.

When it comes to teamwork, I partnered with an office design firm that specializes in creating flexible workspaces. I've never worked with them before, but they come highly recommended. The upper floor of the office building will be co-designed by this company. Staff will be able to easily move furniture on a moment's notice. Most of the walls can be arranged to create private, semiprivate, or open concept workspaces quickly and easily.

The way I positioned the building on the footprint of the land enabled me to make excellent use of available space. Not only did I provide extra-wide doors on the loading dock, I was able to expand the size of the loading dock and add five additional doors. There will be no difficulty getting product into and out of the facility as the company grows.

While I'm providing information about how this building meets their needs, should the model of the building be in plain view or would it be out of view (i.e. covered with a blanket or tarp)? I would cover it. If it's visible, the management team will look at it. They will examine it. They will think about what they're seeing. As they examine and think, they increase their cognitive load. As a result, they're going to have difficulty hearing what I say.

Questions would be encouraged throughout the description.

With the model out of view, questions would be encouraged throughout the description, but I would keep my answers as brief as possible, something we'll discuss during *Step Five*. When I complete my description, I would again ask if there are any questions. Only then would I uncover the model and step back.

There is little value to saying anything at this point. The audience will examine the model, flex their cognitive muscles, think about what I said and reconcile it with what they're now seeing. If I'm a good communicator, I'll stop talking until they're done thinking (or until someone asks a question), regardless of how long it takes. I should not start talking until at least half of them lift their head from the model and look up, although anyone can ask a question at any time.

Whether I use slides to convey my vision of the new building or have a series of posters arranged around the room, I need to follow a similar process. The story surrounding each image needs to be delivered verbally before the image is revealed. When a slide or poster is revealed, it's important to pause, allow them to digest, and answer their questions. Only after all questions about an image are answered do we move to the next. If using posters, I might turn them backwards or cover them before revealing them. With slides, it's possible to use the *b* or *w* key on the keyboard to blank the screen, or place a milestone image between each of the artist's renderings.

This approach accomplishes two things. First, it sets up the audience's cognitive framework in a direction important to their understanding, and it ultimately leads to getting approval for my vision. Second, the information is displayed at a pace appropriate for the audience. Effective face-to-face communication must be two-way and receiver-driven. The speed at which information goes from sender to receiver should be driven by the needs of the receiver, not the sender.

Handouts

Potentially, there are three situations in which handouts could be used: before, during, or after the presentation. When discussion needs to take place around a clear starting point, send the handout in advance. Structure a short five- to ten-minute conversation with the group, similar to what we did with our barking dog presentation. Answer questions throughout the presentation, but keep your answers short. If you send a handout, regardless of whether it's a Microsoft Word or PowerPoint document, assume they've read it when you get together. Do not walk them through the written document they received. Only refer to it when absolutely necessary.

This brings us to another point. We have known since before Johnannes Gutenberg invented movable type more than five hundred years ago that documents printed in a vertical (portrait) format are more readable than those printed in a horizontal (landscape) format. The reason? Line length and eye fatigue. Long lines of text strain your eyes. And when your eyes get to the end of a long line, they have difficulty finding the start of the next line. This makes horizontal presentation decks less readable than traditional, vertical documents. In other words, your documents should be submitted in a vertical format. Use a word processing program to create your handout instead of a slideware program; use Microsoft Word instead of PowerPoint, Pages instead of Keynote.

Using milestones as handouts works very well.

If you feel compelled to provide a handout during your presentation (or you are almost "required" to, such as for a conference), using milestones as handouts works very well. Printed three slides per page, the slides for our barking dog presentation would occupy two sides of a single sheet of paper. Shown below, the handout for the "Present With Ease" presentation developed earlier can be printed two-sided on two sheets of paper.

Presenting
With Ease

Eric Bergman

Best style

Be yourself

_____
_____
_____
_____
_____
_____

Two-way

_____
_____
_____
_____
_____

Receiver-driven

_____
_____
_____
_____
_____

Less is more

_____
_____
_____
_____
_____
_____

People cannot
think and listen

_____
_____
_____
_____
_____

Won't remember
what you say

_____
_____
_____
_____
_____

Be conversational

_____
_____
_____
_____
_____

Think before
you speak

_____
_____
_____
_____
_____

Silence is essential

_____
_____
_____
_____
_____

There is ample room to take notes. Everyone has a basic road map. It's up to them to fill it in along the way. You'll notice, for example, that the diagram of the pattern of face-to-face communication is not included in the handout. As discussed, it has been left out to encourage participants to draw the diagram themselves as it's revealed in the presentation, thereby encouraging participation. By the way, the original font size for these slides is 144-point.

At the end of these "Present With Ease" sessions, participants receive a detailed, written description of the principles (a shortened version of the next chapter) they can access a number of ways. I often bring hard copies for participants to pick up at the end of the presentation. Alternatively, I may e-mail the .pdf document to participants, or provide a link on my website from which they can download the .pdf. With this two-step approach, the audience receives two handouts, one during the presentation and one afterwards, neither of which interferes with the conversation.

Whiteboards & Flip Charts

Drawing pictures, creating diagrams, and jotting down notes on a whiteboard, flip chart, or piece of paper can be excellent tools to communicate effectively. Many salespeople have told me over the years that they draw diagrams for clients during sales presentations. They have also said clients often ask if they can keep the piece of paper on which the diagram was drawn. The reason? Clients participate in the creation of the visual. Chances are, they'll be able to look at every squiggle on the page and remember the part of the conversation from which it emanated. This is engagement.

The first time I delivered a presentation on "Five Steps to Conquer Death by PowerPoint," I used a flip chart. I was testing some ideas in a group presentation and didn't want to spend any time creating slides. When I wrote "1. Put the audience first," one of the participants said, "You could have put that on a slide." Later, however, when we examined the question-and-answer process, I received information from the group on the length of their presentations and the average number of questions asked during those presentations. I pointed out that it would have been impossible to put that information on a slide because it came from that particular group, and every group's input is different.

We have moved away from drawing pictures, and we need to move back.

We have moved away from drawing pictures, and we need to move back. Whiteboards used to be a staple of most meeting rooms, boardrooms, and training rooms. More recently, these tools have been replaced with screens and projectors. However, thanks to technology, the concept of drawing pictures during presentations is making a comeback in a couple of ways. The first is smart boards, which are essentially electronic whiteboards. You can draw pictures and create images, and it's easy to save the images to a file for circulation later. The second is whiteboard applications on tablet computers. Both of these can and should be thought of as effective communication tools.

There are a number of advantages to drawing pictures. First and foremost, the visuals are drawn at a pace that's perfect for the audience. Second, this helps the presenter adhere to the principle of less is more, which we'll examine in greater detail during *Step Four*. Third, the information drawn can be gleaned from the audience, making it directly appropriate to their needs. They're engaged because they are helping to create the visual.

Using PowerPoint One-on-One

I read an interesting blog item from sales consultant Geoffrey James on using PowerPoint one-on-one during sales presentations. "Sales reps have a term for the standard corporate presentation," he writes. "Death by PowerPoint. They also have a term for sales reps who try to use [these prepackaged presentations] with customers: unemployed."[ix]

His first advice for salespeople is quite simple: "Stop using PowerPoint." To successfully communicate, salespeople should do their homework, create an agenda, focus on the customer, and close on next steps. Interestingly, this advice sounds a lot like the five steps on which this book is based.

A number of years ago, a client of mine, who ran a venture capital fund at the time, asked that I spend a day with his marketing director to enhance her presentation skills. Most of their presentations were one-on-one or to small groups of investment advisors with specific types of clients who could invest in the venture capital fund.

I spent most of the day with her, during which her skills and confidence increased significantly. At the end of the day, he came into the room and said: "Eric, I know your feelings on PowerPoint, but we have this presentation that we've put together to use one-on-one with advisors. I'd like your opinion on it."

Sigh.

Addictions can be difficult to overcome, even at the best of times.

Addictions can be difficult to overcome, even at the best of times. I agreed to go along, but I made a suggestion for proceeding. We would sit across the table from her to simulate presenting to one or two people—i.e. one or two advisors. We would video record the presentation. For the first five minutes, the marketing director would deliver the presentation from her laptop with the screen in plain view for everyone. For the second five minutes, she would turn the laptop around so we couldn't see it and talk to us, using what she sees on the screen as notes to structure her side of the conversation.

At the end of ten minutes, I stopped recording, turned to him, and asked: "Do you even want to play back the recordings?"

"No," he said. "That won't be necessary. You really like being right, don't you?"

"Yes," I replied, smiling. "I just wish my family was here to hear it."

The difference between the two versions was nothing short of amazing. During the first five minutes, all three of us were distracted by what was on the screen. She was having difficulty focusing; we were having difficulty listening. During the last five minutes, she simply glanced at the screen to get her next idea, lifted her head to think about that idea, and then expressed it clearly and concisely. She communicated more effectively; we could simply focus on listening. Interestingly, during the second five minutes, we also asked questions that she answered clearly and concisely. We came to the conclusion that it was difficult to ask questions during the first five minutes because PowerPoint got in the way.

Using "Off-the-Shelf" Presentations

A number of organizations use PowerPoint to develop standard off-the-shelf or stock presentations. The idea is that the same message will be delivered to each audience. The problem with this approach is that every audience is different. Stock presentations tend to completely ignore *Step One*. The audience doesn't come first, the message does.

Often, stock presentations are developed as part of an overall branding exercise. The logic seems to be that by using consistent color schemes and logos, the organization's brand will be burned into the conscious thought and subconscious existence of the audience. However, I don't think this works nearly as well as hoped.

For more than ten years, I conducted rookie advisor training for a brokerage firm. For most of that time, I asked advisors to name the last three mutual fund wholesalers who delivered group presentations to their branches. At least 99 percent of the time, not one advisor in the room could name three. When we probed, the reason was easy to determine. These wholesalers all blended together. Not one stood out as memorable. They all undoubtedly used PowerPoint. So much for the branding argument and the ability to set your organization apart.

Even if the stock presentation serves a specific purpose, there's little chance that you'll be able to shuffle and/or remove some slides and be ready to present to an audience. When the stock presentation was created, whoever developed it was saying "this information was perfect when it left our hands."

But how it left their hands has nothing to do with the audience you're facing. Your job is to ensure that the information in your presentation is tailored to their needs. The only thing that counts is whether the audience applies or acts on the information you deliver.

However, the true value of off-the-shelf presentations is the wealth of information they contain. In fact, they almost always contain too much. Your challenge will undoubtedly be to remove information from the original presentation, regardless of the audience, which underscores the value of the approach discussed in this book. Once you complete your analysis of need, value and audience, and assemble your basic presentation framework and notes, your challenge is to find information from the stock presentation that fits your framework and your outline. Everything else can be saved for other presentations as appropriate.

This is very similar to the speechwriting challenges I faced. Only after the outline was complete (and approved), would I turn to the mountain of information provided to find the pieces that fit it— facts, statistics, anecdotes, stories, examples, and, as a very last step, charts and graphs.

If you follow a similar process with off-the-shelf presentations, you enhance your ability to structure meaningful, relevant conversations with audiences. Include only those parts directly relevant to that specific audience. Do not blindly copy and paste slides from one presentation to another. Ignore information that does not fit your outline, or save it for another presentation to another audience at another time.

Visuals Are a Spice

Visuals are a spice. Like any spice, they can add flavor. Used in excess, they can quickly ruin the meal. If appropriate to the message and properly used, and if the proper tool is applied, visual aids can assist communication. Conversely, if visuals are overused or inappropriate to the message, or if the wrong tool is selected, they can hinder the transfer of information and knowledge.

If it doesn't add to the conversation,
it subtracts from it.

If a visual—any visual—does not contribute to the communication process, it takes away from overall effectiveness. If it doesn't add to the conversation, it subtracts from it. There's no middle ground with visual aids, especially slides.

Before developing your visuals, outline your strategy, complete your basic presentation framework and develop your notes. Do not let the tool dictate how you communicate. Develop visual aids to supplement your notes, not the other way around.

To avoid 'Death by PowerPoint', every slide you use must add value. If you wouldn't be willing to make a donation to charity for every slide you're thinking of using, you have to ask yourself if it's really necessary. While you must minimize visual aids to enhance effectiveness—especially the use of slides—you should also expand the range of tools you use. There are a variety of tools available, and you should select the appropriate tool for the need. Draw diagrams. Bring props when appropriate. You don't need PowerPoint to show a YouTube clip. Use the best tool for the job to enhance your success. However, if you're ever in doubt, omit the visuals or blank the screen and simply talk to your audience.

Step Four:
Convey Your Message & Personality

The first three steps to conquering 'Death by PowerPoint' have primarily focused on developing strategy and content for presentations. The last two steps are all about delivery.

When delivering a presentation of any kind, whether one-on-one or to a room of a thousand, it's important that you achieve two goals. You must convey your message. Within your message, there must be a call to action. We've discussed that a number of times. If you don't want the audience to apply or take action on your information, why are you there?

But to be effective, you must also convey your personality, who you are as an individual and/or a professional. If people don't believe you're sincere, you won't convince them of much, whether they're sitting across from you one-on-one or in the back row of an auditorium filled with 999 of their peers. If the medium is the message, your personality (not your PowerPoint or Keynote slides) must be the window through which the message must travel to be received, understood, and acted upon by the audience.

Relaxed conversation is your
best possible presentation style.

Each of us conveys our message and personality every day of our lives when we're engaged in a relaxed conversation. It doesn't matter whether we're delivering a sales presentation to a prospect or a plenary session at a major conference; message and personality must work together to achieve the greatest success. The basic premise here is that relaxed conversation is our best possible presentation style. It is also the first of ten fundamental principles we'll examine in this chapter.

I once had an interesting experience that illustrates the importance of message and personality working together. I was conducting a two-day training program for a financial services organization. At the end of the second day, one of the participants came up to tell me she had conducted a financial seminar for female professionals the previous week and had invited two speakers, an accountant, and a lawyer. In her mind, the accountant did everything right. He showed up early, ensured the projector was working and delivered his PowerPoint presentation. He presented a virtual mountain of information. He went a bit over his allotted time, and there were very few questions, but the woman telling me the story assumed that was because the information was so clear.

The lawyer barely arrived in time. He sat casually in a chair while the accountant went through his presentation. When it was his turn to speak, the lawyer pulled his chair to the front of the room, turned off the projector, sat down and started talking to the group. At one point, he even brought over another chair, over which he draped his arm.

"He was slouching," she said. She was offended that the lawyer didn't take the seminar seriously enough even to sit up straight.

The lawyer referred to the accountant's presentation a few times, which led my client to believe that the lawyer didn't take time to prepare a presentation (and led me to think that the accountant had prepared more than enough information for two!). People were encouraged not only to talk about their particular situation in general terms, but also to ask questions throughout. Basically, the lawyer created an extended conversation with the group.

And they responded appropriately. At the end of the evening, evaluation forms were distributed. The results shocked her. "The lawyer scored so much higher than the accountant on the evaluations," she told me. "When I saw the evaluations, I couldn't believe it. He wasn't prepared. He slouched. He broke every rule in the book.

He didn't present.
He conversed.

"I couldn't understand why people responded to the lawyer's presentation the way they did. But after attending your workshop, I now understand. He didn't present. He conversed, and the participants got more value from the conversation than from the presentation that preceded it."

Adult learners get more out of the information transfer process when they're treated as peers—accepted and respected as intelligent, experienced individuals whose opinions are listened to, honored, and appreciated.[x] This concept could and should be applied to all presentations. If there isn't someone with slightly more knowledge about a topic (the presenter) or people with somewhat less knowledge (the audience), why conduct the presentation in the first place? But we can't ignore the knowledge and experience of others. Certainly, the presenter is supposed to have knowledge or information to share. But the more equal the footing between presenter and audience and the greater the participation by the audience, the better the learning experience from everyone's perspective. Such an approach would be both two-way and symmetrical. In other words, it's a conversation.

Conversations Have Value

This chapter is dedicated to examining conversations and transferring that examination to group presentations, so you can conduct extended conversations with all audiences. It is designed to help you understand the skills you've developed one-on-one, and provide you with a framework for enhancing those skills and applying them to the challenge of delivering your ideas to groups. We're going to examine fundamental principles of relaxed conversation that are focused on how people can effectively receive information orally, and how you can communicate more effectively to aid their understanding.

These principles do not change whether you're talking to one person or a thousand. They also do not change on the basis of language, gender, age, ethnocultural origin, sexual orientation, level of physical ability, or position of power within an organization. If you understand these principles and learn to apply them effectively, you will become a better communicator. Logically, the more effective you are as a communicator, the more effectively you can deliver your ideas to one person or many, and manage the communication process to win-win outcomes.

So what are these principles? An important one is that face-to-face com-munication must be two-way. Indeed, as we'll explore, all communication must be two-way. If it isn't two-way, it isn't communication. This is so simple and logical that often we don't even think about it. But this simple principle has all but disappeared from modern presentations.

Decks become behemoths,
and we become their slaves.

Today, it's possible to download mountains of information into a slideware program. The result? Decks become behemoths, and we become their slaves. The information becomes more important than the understanding it's sup-posed to generate. As we have previously discussed, people assume that because they have said something during a presentation or a specific piece of infor-mation was shown on a slide, they have communicated. Yet nothing could be further from the truth.

There is no communication unless something comes back. In some way, the receiver of information must send a message to the sender. It's the only way to determine whether the message was received and understood, and whether it might be applied or acted upon.

In a presentation, if you're communicating with the audience in a conver-sational style, you should see them thinking about the ideas you convey. They should be concentrating on what you're saying, nodding their heads when they understand, or showing a puzzled expression if they don't. If most of them look puzzled, should you continue? Or should you ask if anyone has a ques-tion? In a conversation you would stop and answer questions, as you should during your presentations.

Granted, there are a couple of differences in communicating to groups, compared to a one-on-one conversation. But there are a great many similari-ties —perhaps more than you might imagine. Occasionally, you might get away with less preparation one-on-one, but you won't get away with it when you're presenting to groups. You must have a plan.

When presenting to groups, you need to learn to manage nervousness and adrenaline. Interestingly, during twenty years of coaching others, I've discovered that the best way to reduce nervousness is to encourage questions throughout your presentation, which transforms it from a presentation to a conversation. It's the most calming thing you can do when talking to a group. But to be successful, as we'll discuss during *Step Five*, your answers must be brief.

In all presentations, it's important to create a two-way exchange, even though you'll do most of the talking. You must use the appropriate visual tool to aid communication, not as a crutch on which you lean. And you must always display enthusiasm appropriate to the situation. If you're announcing a layoff, for example, your level of enthusiasm will be different than if you're introducing a new product to your distribution network or a new service to your customers.

The following principles will help you communicate more effectively, whether you're having a conversation or delivering a presentation. Bottom line? If your audience does not understand your information, cannot apply it, or does not take action on it, you've ultimately wasted their time and yours. And that's what 'Death by PowerPoint' is all about.

Principle #1 — Your best style is relaxed conversation

Every time you stand in front of a group to deliver a presentation, you must achieve two basic goals. First, you need to convey a message. If you don't have a message to contribute, no value to offer the audience, then why stand there in the first place? Second, you need to convey your personality—who you are as an individual and a professional. If the medium is the message, your personality is the window through which the message must travel to be received, understood, and acted upon by the audience.

> *Each of us conveys our message*
> *and our personality every day.*

Each of us conveys our message and our personality every day of our life in relaxed conversation. It doesn't matter whether we're talking to a friend, a family member, a client, a colleague, or a prospect. When we talk to someone else one-on-one, the other person gets a sense not only of our message but also of the person delivering it.

Relaxed conversation is, therefore, our best possible communication style. Instead of trying to learn a new range of skills to present to groups, why not build on the skills we already possess? Think of the best speakers you've seen or the best presentations you've attended. What made them effective? Their slides? No, for most of us it's the feeling they're talking to each of us directly, even if we're in a room with a thousand other people.

During a conversation, think of what happens when one friend is explaining a concept to another. The first person is doing most of the talking. He or she is enthusiastic, so the words come tumbling out; the rate of word delivery is rapid.

But there are many pauses. The sender pauses to think before speaking. After conveying each idea, he or she watches the receiver carefully, looking for nods and listening for "uh-huhs" that signal the receiver has internalized one piece of information and is ready to receive the next. Sometimes, pauses occur in the middle of a phrase or sentence. They may last four or five seconds. If the receiver looks puzzled at any point, the sender will probably backtrack, side-track, or stop. He or she may ask if there are any questions. Once a question or series of questions is answered and a "milestone of mutual understanding" is created, the sender gets back on track and moves the conversation forward. In conversation, most of us know there's no sense moving forward if the person we're talking to has no idea of where we are.

Milestones of mutual understanding occur frequently in good conversations. They should become just as frequent in your presentations.

You must emulate conversations during your presentations.

To do that, you must emulate conversations during your presentations. You're not there to "download" data. You're there to put information in perspective, create understanding based on a two-way exchange, and facilitate an environment in which people can apply what you tell them to their personal or professional lives.

You will have a structured plan for your side of the conversation. But you shouldn't plod through your plan at the expense of the audience; you cannot ignore their perspective or their side of the conversation. If you see a puzzled expression at any time, handle it in a manner similar to how you would in a conversation. Ask if there are any questions. And you don't need to single the person out. Simply ask the group if there is something you can explain more effectively. Then pause and wait.

Whenever possible, encourage questions throughout your presentations. But be brief with your answers. Questions are an opportunity to create milestones of mutual understanding. But remember, you pass milestones. You don't camp at them.

Principle #2 — Be yourself

You are unique. You have your own way of speaking and your own mannerisms. How you talk, how you stand, how you hold your hands is part of your body language, and yours alone. If you stifle your natural gestures or attempt to adopt new gestures when you stand in front of a group, you run a high risk of coming across as plastic, contrived, or phony. Any of these will make it difficult for the audience to trust you. And at that point, your message won't matter.

You know there are certain standards you must meet when delivering a presentation. You need to dress appropriately. The right level of formality is important. You might be more relaxed at a small staff meeting than with the organization's board of directors. Formality aside, however, your body language must be natural. What's natural for you is probably unnatural for someone else, and vice-versa. This is why it's important to question and often completely ignore the "rules" we've all encountered for body language and the use of gestures.

For example, consider the generally-accepted taboo of crossing your arms. A few years ago, I conducted media training for an organization that was facing a potential strike. The training was for management-level employees who might be called upon to deal with journalists at strike sites. Prior to the media training portion of the agenda, the company's director of human resources spent about forty-five minutes talking to the group about the logistics of managing the strike. She was a very good communicator.

Later, when we discussed body language in broadcast interviews and presentations of all types, I crossed my arms and asked if this was appropriate body language. Everyone said, "No, it is inappropriate." They told me that someone looks closed when they do that. Interestingly, in more than twenty years of looking, I have never been able to uncover a single piece of research to verify this generally accepted belief.

I turned to the HR director and asked if she would ever stand in front of a group and present information or answer questions with her arms crossed. She said she would not. I asked the group of twenty-plus people if she would ever do that, and they all said that she was far too professional to ever cross her arms while standing in front of a group.

I recorded her with her arms crossed during her presentation.

However, that was exactly what she had done when she presented to this group. I was sitting at the back of the room, with my video camera on a tripod, so I recorded her with her arms crossed during her presentation. When I played back the video recording, everyone was surprised that they didn't notice she had committed what is often known as a body language "sin."

The point I made to this group was that, because the HR director was communicating effectively and naturally as herself, they didn't even mentally record the body language. It was natural for her; her body language was consistent with who she is as a person. And what's natural for her would be unnatural for someone else. If she had been standing outside the room having a conversation with someone, her arms might just as likely be crossed, but she'd be listening with the attentiveness that only a human resources professional can display.

The Mehrabian Myth—Body Language Advice Gone Wrong

One of the most ubiquitous sources of research on body language has perhaps become the most misquoted statistic in human history. It comes from a book called *Silent Messages*, written by Albert Mehrabian and first published in 1971. The statistic most often misquoted goes something like this:

- 55 percent of the overall message is how the person looks when delivering the message.

- 38 percent of the overall message is how the person sounds when delivering the message.

- 7 percent of the overall message consists of the words themselves.

Professor Mehrabian's original research, as published, bears no resemblance to the statistics stated above. A blog article I published in 2004 entitled "The Mehrabian Myth" has since spawned a virtual cottage industry, including one highly entertaining animated video on YouTube. According to the Google Analytics on my website, the term "Mehrabian Myth" (or a slight variation of it) is now searched at least twenty times per month.

The way Mehrabian is misquoted seems to state that if you're watching two people converse in a foreign language, you should be able to listen to how the words sound, watch their gestures and get 93 percent of the message. However, this is not the case. You'll recognize emotion, but if you don't understand the words, you receive significantly less than 93 percent of what transpires.

During the past forty-plus years, misquoted Mehrabian statistics have formed the basis for misguided advice on body language during speeches, presentations, and television interviews. If 55 percent of the message is how you look when you say the words, as this misinformed advice tells us, we should be able to create the right image with that 55 percent. "Hold your hands this way," this advice says. "Use open gestures. Don't do this. Don't do that."

Those who have read *Silent Messages* (or at least have read all of Chapter Three of it) know that Professor Mehrabian is not talking about creating or contriving body language. Instead, he states his belief that words, voice, and body language must be consistent. If they are inconsistent, the receiver of the information relies on more than spoken words to evaluate the overall message. As the professor writes, "when actions contradict words, people rely more heavily on actions to infer another's feelings."[xi] In other words, if you try to create body language in your presentations, the people receiving your message will sense it and not trust what you're saying, because your actions will contradict your words.

*Most body language advice tells us
to be anything but natural.*

Most body language advice tells us to be anything but natural. One pundit says don't cross your arms or legs, relax your shoulders, don't touch your face, keep your head up, and use your hands more confidently.[xii] Another tells us that it's of great significance for you to control your nonverbal messages as much as your verbal ones.[xiii]

Make no mistake, when you try to contrive or control body language, people sense it. The cognitive reason for this is that rehearsed body language occurs after the words are spoken, as opposed to what happens during relaxed conversation, in which natural body language emerges before you say the words.[xiv] This creates a disconnect for the listener and casts doubt on what you're saying. If anything, this emphasizes the importance of being yourself, which is the only way to ensure consistency between the words spoken, how they sound when they're spoken, and how the person looks when they're spoken.

Work of Psycholinguists

When seeking body language advice for presentations, perhaps the best place to look is in the work of psycholinguists. Psycholinguists study the psychological and neurobiological factors that enable humans to acquire, use, and understand language.[xv] It has been a recognized field of social psychology for about fifty years.

Professor David McNeill of the University of Chicago is a psycholinguist who has been studying nonverbal communication for more than thirty years. In his studies, he has concluded that people communicate best when they create unconscious and spontaneous gestures. They key words here are "unconscious" and "spontaneous." If you clasp your hands rigidly behind your back because you don't know what to do with them, you are neither "unconscious" nor "spontaneous." You're simply not being yourself. If you're not being yourself, you are not communicating your personality. And if you don't convey your personality, the audience will be skeptical of your message.

In her book *Hearing Gesture: How Our Hands Help Us Think*, psycholinguist Susan Goldin-Meadow points out that no culture has been discovered in which people do not move their hands as they talk. And as Dr. Goldin-Meadow has discovered, a person speaking does not even have to be sighted to use gestures. In her book, she describes an experiment in which children and teens blind from birth participated in a series of conversational tasks. All of the children used gestures. "The blind group gestured at the same rate as the sighted group," she writes, "and conveyed the same information using the same range of gesture forms." Regardless of our culture or language, we all use gestures to help us think and communicate.

Most of us intuitively know this. According to Dr. Goldin-Meadow: "Several types of evidence lend support to the view that gesture and speech form a single, unified system. The gestures speakers produce along with their talk are symbolic acts that convey meaning." This is why we get more out of face-to-face meetings than from telephone conversations.

The evidence also indicates that gestures make it easier to think.

The evidence also indicates that gestures make it easier to think. "When the act of speaking becomes difficult, speakers seem to respond by increasing their gestures," Dr. Goldin-Meadow writes. Her hypothesis is that gesturing reduces demands on a speaker's cognitive resources. Attempting to reduce or eliminate gestures (i.e. by being told not to gesture as much by a psycholinguist conducting an experiment or, potentially, by a presentation consultant trying to get you to convey the "right image") makes it more difficult to think of what you're trying to say at the times you need all your wits about you.

Professor Goldin-Meadow believes that to "ignore gesture is to ignore part of the conversation."[xvi] Her research has led her to the conclusion that first, the act of gesturing facilitates communication by promoting spatial thinking, and that, second, attempts to stifle gestures inhibit someone's ability to think.[xvii] "At the very least," she says, "we ought to stop telling people not to move their hands when they talk."[xviii]

Quite frankly, if you use gestures when you're engaged in a conversation on the telephone (and virtually all of us do), you should bring those gestures to your presentations and let them happen naturally. They're an integral component of who you are as a human being and, therefore, fundamental to the concept of "being yourself."

Using gestures naturally is the best possible way to ensure consistency between the words spoken, how they sound when they're spoken, and how you look when they're spoken. Natural gestures enhance your ability to think on your feet. And in such a scenario, words and actions will be consistent with each other, allowing your audience to focus on what you're saying instead of what you're doing with your hands.

Be yourself while having a conversation with the audience. Focus on communicating effectively. The gestures will take care of themselves, and your effectiveness at influencing others will be strengthened.

Principle #3 — Relaxed conversation is two-way

Let's examine a basic communication model. On one side, we have a sender, who encodes a message, where it's sent out along a medium and, ultimately, decoded by the receiver. This model illustrates the concept.

However, this is not communication. It's a one-way transmission of information. There's no communication until something comes back, which is how communication acts as a catalyst for creating a shared reality between sender(s) and receiver(s). The receiver has to encode a message and send it along a medium, where it is decoded by the original sender. To be true communication, the process should look very similar to the next model.

A shared reality is best created through a back-and-forth exchange. If we look at texting, bulletin boards, electronic messenger services, and e-mail conversations, we see a constant flow between sender and receiver in both directions. The best conversations, whether in-person or via text message, are those in which both sides play a role, with the ultimate goal of enhancing understanding. This is two-way and symmetrical.

Your presentations, like your conversations, must be two-way. If you treat people with respect and create a two-way process in which they can absorb your information and you can answer their questions clearly and concisely, you stand a better chance of having them apply or act on your message than if you stand in front of them and dump data while talking to your slides.

Principle #4 — Relaxed conversation is receiver-driven

In a relaxed conversation, the speed at which information goes from sender to receiver is driven by the receiver's needs, not the sender's. If the receiver doesn't signal understanding with a nod or by saying "uh-huh," the sender should stop before moving on. If the sender fails to stop, one of two things happens. The receiver either keeps thinking about the previous idea and misses the new one or stops thinking about the old idea (thereby forgetting it) and simply tries to keep up.

If you're sitting with your boss or explaining a marketing idea to a colleague, you need to send information at a rate based on that person's need to understand, not your need to get through it all in a prescribed time.

If you talk nonstop,
you'll quickly lose your audience.

The same applies to your presentations. If you talk nonstop, you'll quickly lose your audience, even if you have something interesting to say. You will resemble the person at a party who has cornered someone and talks their ear off. Of course, the more the first person talks, the less the second person actually listens. And it's quite likely that the less he or she listens, the more the first person talks.

Is it possible to be completely receiver-driven with an audience? I believe it is, but not if you use slides. In the mid-1990s, I worked with a trust company that conducted estate planning seminars. The company's marketing department sent out a thick binder of acetates to sales representatives so they could conduct seminars at retail branches.

One of their trust officers was extremely effective at turning these seminars into business for the firm by completely ignoring the acetates. His strategy was simple. He started his seminars with the usual introductions and thank-yous, then stood beside a flipchart and said to the group: "I bet you folks have a lot of questions about will and estate planning. What I'd like to do is write down your questions right up front on this flipchart, so we make sure I answer all of them during my presentation." He gently cajoled the group until they started asking questions. It never took long.

He wrote down their questions on the flipchart. Sometimes he would have four or five pages filled with questions. Some of them he would answer right away. Should everyone have a will? Yes. He would write the answer directly underneath the question.

He would then deliver his presentation. He had a plan. The visuals he used were the ones he created on the flip chart as his presentation unfolded. Going through information, he would refer to the flip chart as questions were answered, adjusting his information slightly to meet the group's needs as the presentation unfolded. At the end of his presentation, he went question by question through his list and made sure every one was answered.

His presentations were extremely effective. Clients responded very positively. More importantly, they brought their business. His seminars generated significant identifiable business for the company.

I have used this technique with fantastic success over the years. It's two-way. It's receiver-driven. If handled effectively, it works very well. But it cannot be achieved within the rigid structure of PowerPoint or Keynote.

In your presentations, make sure the information you're sending is driven by audience needs, not yours. If they're thinking about an idea you've just expressed, stop talking until they absorb it. If you don't, even if there's a high degree of audience interest in what you're talking about, they'll remember very little about what you've said.

If you express an idea that creates puzzled expressions, it's a good time to stop and ask: "Are there any questions?" You would do this in conversation. You should also do this with your presentations. In fact, with groups of fifty or fewer participants, there's no reason for not answering questions at all times throughout your presentations.

Principle #5 — Less is more

There is a paradox in face-to-face communication: The less you say, the more your audience remembers. I actually tested this concept with a project I was working on with a pharmaceutical company.

The less you say,
the more your audience remembers.

The project encouraged vaccination of young women for the human pappillomavirus (HPV). We were preparing for a presentation to a national pediatric society, the goal of which was to provide physicians with communication strategies they could apply to their individual practices. We set up a clinical scenario to video record a mother and her thirteen-year-old daughter during a regular visit to the doctor. The physician broached the topic of HPV vaccination. Generally, a physician has less than five minutes to introduce a new topic and answer questions. In this instance, he introduced the topic and, in two-and-a-half minutes, answered five questions. His answers were long. The parent said she would discuss the concept with her spouse over dinner that night and they would make a decision.

After this, everyone took a break from video recording. The group chatted among themselves, but I took our physician off to the side to discuss the concept of being receiver-driven and keeping his answers as short as possible. I even introduced the ten-pushup rule, which we'll discuss in greater detail in the next chapter. But for now, let's just say he was encouraged to keep all of his answers to ten words or less.

We brought the mother and daughter back in and asked them what they remembered about the earlier discussion. To say they remembered very little is an understatement. The physician was shocked at how little they retained. There's no way they could have had an informed discussion with the other spouse over dinner.

We went through the process a second time. The subject was introduced and both mother and daughter started asking questions. They asked nine questions in less than one-and-one-half minutes. Initially, the physician felt terrible, believing he didn't tell them a thing. However, the mother and daughter got to ask the questions and explore the issues that were important to their understanding.

We broke for lunch. After lunch, we brought the mother and daughter back in and asked them what they remembered from the second approach. The difference in their understanding absolutely astounded the physician, even though we all agreed it wasn't a fair test since they had already heard the information once. But they could easily have had an informed discussion with the other parent over dinner. On camera, I asked the physician what he thought.

"I thought that answering questions in a short form was going to be too abrupt," he said. "My own feeling is that I like to explain when I give an answer and go into more detail. But afterwards, seeing how they responded to short answers to their questions and the information they had gathered, they seemed to get more information with short answers. This was very interesting and very revealing to me."

"I can feel more confident giving short answers."

"I can feel more confident giving short answers and not going into a lot of detail. I always thought that if I didn't give them enough information, I was being derelict in my duties. But if I see them retaining more information, then perhaps that's the way to go."

From this physician's perspective, this is actually quite easy to test. For two weeks, he could alternate the old way with the new when introducing a concept to patients and encouraging them to ask questions. For the first week, the physician could provide longer answers, as he has done for twenty-five-plus years. For the second, he could keep every answer to ten words or less, or one word if "yes" or "no" is all that's required. Make a note in the chart about whether the patient belongs to the first group (more information through longer answers) or the second group (less information through shorter answers). When they return, briefly ask them what they remember from the last conversation. Grade their level of understanding on a scale from one to ten and decide which is more effective.

Similarly, if you try to cram too much information into your presentations, you won't create a two-way exchange. And you certainly won't be receiver-driven. How could you be? The speed at which information travels from you to the audience is not driven by their need for understanding, but your need to get through it all within a certain time period. If you have one hour allotted for your presentation, bring no more than thirty to thirty-five minutes of information. This allows you to adhere to the principle of "less is more" and answer questions along the way. Provided your answers are brief, you'll get through your information in the allotted time. And if you finish five minutes early, who will complain?

Principle #6 — People can listen or they can think

Of all the principles I teach, this one has caused the most controversy over the years. I cannot begin to count the number of times people have challenged this principle. But the more it's challenged, the more I'm convinced that, as human beings, we can listen or we can think, but we cannot listen and think at the same time.

It doesn't matter whether you're male or female, old or young. If you're thinking about something, you cannot take more information into your working memory; you cannot listen. If you're talking on your mobile phone while driving your car along the freeway and there are no problems with traffic, of course you can carry on the conversation. But if something happens in front of you, you have a choice. You can devote your attention to the conversation or what's in front of you. You cannot do both.

In the 1990s, a North American insurance organization conducted a study on cell phone use and driving. People were given an obstacle course to navigate. They went through the course the first time while focusing on their driving. They were given a score (i.e. number of cones touched) and timed. The second time, they were given a mobile phone and were told they had to continue a conversation while navigating the obstacle course. When the results were released, the scientist conducting the study started the news conference by saying "we have proven that people cannot listen and think at the same time."

A number of years ago, I conducted some training for YMCA at one of their internal conferences in Montreal, Quebec. My session was on a Saturday morning, and my client asked if I'd like to stay over Saturday night (it was back in the days when staying over a Saturday night actually meant cheaper flights). At their dinner wrap-up that evening, they were bringing in a motivational speaker. I ran this past my spouse, who said it was OK with her if I stayed over in Montreal on a Saturday night.

The speaker was great; she was very enthusiastic and she made a lot of excellent points. In her introduction, she told us she had come from a poor background, had earned her Ph.D., and was looking after her sister's children. She had many interesting things to say, and I kept thinking "Wow, I can really use that in my business." But there were absolutely no pauses in her presentation. As soon as one great idea came out, it was quickly followed by another, and so on.

When I got home the next day, my spouse asked me if I enjoyed the speaker. "She was great," I said, meaning it.

"What did she talk about?"

"She told us she came from a poor background, earned her Ph.D., and was now looking after her sister's children," I replied.

"So what did she talk about?"

For the life of me, I couldn't remember a single additional detail. As I struggled to remember, I could tell by the look on my wife's face that she didn't believe I went to dinner with my client. To this day, I suspect she believes I skipped the dinner to spend a wild Saturday night in Montreal.

They cannot think and listen at the same time.

The audiences to which you present are just like you and me. They cannot think and listen at the same time. By definition, this means that you must pause when delivering your presentations. And those pauses must be as full and as frequent in your presentations as they are in your conversations.

You want your information to be thought provoking. However, don't disturb those thoughts when you provoke them. You want people to think about what you're saying and apply it to their personal or professional situation. They need to take your information and transfer it from working memory to long-term memory. But while they're engaged in that process, they won't hear a word you say if you continue talking. Alternatively, if you disturb their thinking process, they won't internalize your information.

Principle #7 — People won't remember what you say

Anyone with a spouse, partner, or significant other knows that people won't remember what you say. Instead, they'll remember what they thought about what you said. People at your presentations will not remember your exact words. They will remember what they thought about what you said—how they took your information and applied it to their individual frame of reference. It is this process that truly makes face-to-face communication effective, especially if your information is attached to who they are as human beings.

But this process can only occur in silence, whether you give them that silence or they take it for themselves. And remember, if they take that silence to think about a previous idea while you're talking about the next one, they can't hear a word you're saying.

If your pace is effective and you allow the audience the time they need to take what you say and compare it to who they are as individuals, they'll remember your message over the long term. This is where communication really works, whether one-on-one or to groups, and it underscores the importance of telling stories, not dumping data, during your presentations. By applying this principle, you can improve your communication effectiveness during both group and one-on-one presentations.

Principle #8 — Be conversational in your delivery

If you've ever read the transcript of an interview or conversation, you've probably noticed that people rarely talk in complete sentences. If you participated in the conversation from which the transcript was drawn, you were probably shocked at what you saw written down. It makes much more sense when you hear it than when you read it later on.

There is a basic pattern that occurs during relaxed conversation. It begins when the sender thinks about what he or she is going to say (I think). This is the first pause. As difficult as it is during your presentation, even with adrenaline coursing through your veins, you must think, in silence, about each idea before you deliver it. Once the idea is formed, the sender expresses it (I talk). If the sender is enthusiastic, the words come tumbling out at a rapid rate of word delivery.

There are two elements of pace
in spoken communication.

This brings us to an important point. There are two elements of pace in spoken communication: rate-of-word-delivery and rate of ideas. Many times, presenters are advised to slow down. The ... way ... people ... often ... respond ... to ... this ... advice ... is ... to ... slow ... down ... their ... rate ... of ... word ... delivery. This is what happens when you hear someone drone on in a monotone. Never slow down your rate-of-word-delivery. Get the words out quickly if you wish to be conversational. But pause between ideas. This gives people an opportunity to internalize what you're saying.

Once you deliver the idea, stop talking and allow the receiver to think about what was just said (They think). The receiver needs this pause to absorb the idea and relate it to a meaningful frame of reference. During this second pause, watch and listen for the receiver's reaction (I watch/listen). Once there's a nod or "uh-huh," you can form the next idea (I think). And the process repeats itself.

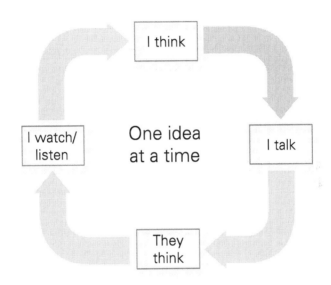

If you start watching people around you during conversations, you'll discover that this cycle occurs less than twenty words at a time. A similar pattern should occur during your presentations. However, this can be difficult if adrenaline is driving the process. Under the influence of adrenaline, it's possible for pauses to be two, three, ten, or even twenty minutes apart, especially if you don't adhere to the principle of "less is more" and bring too much information to begin with. When this happens, the information becomes a non-stop stream that can be extremely difficult for the audience to absorb.

Audiences are used to hearing and participating in conversations. We all receive information in that format every single day. We need pauses to absorb the information. If someone prepares a speech and reads it to us, or talks nonstop off the top of his or her head, we tune out. On the speech side, as soon as we hear perfect sentence structure we know we're being read to, not communicated with. On the nonstop talking side, we can't keep up, so we give up.

Delivering Presentations from Notes

This is one of the reasons for my recommendation that you use notes to deliver your presentations. Each note should be a balance between a written script (speech) and no notes (ad-lib, off-the-cuff, or memorization) that represents up to twenty words that actually come out of your mouth. Notes are six to ten word reminders of each full idea, similar to what we did earlier for our barking dog presentation in both the five-minute and ten-minute formats.

Don't show your notes to the audience.

Unless you're quoting someone directly, there need not be a grammatically correct sentence in your notes. And let's be clear. Projecting your notes onto a screen as bullet points, or handing them out as a presentation deck that you can talk to will not increase your success. You should use notes to structure your side of the conversation, but have them in front of you. Don't show them to the audience.

Each note should represent up to twenty words of speaking. To deliver a note, glance down quickly to read it, then look up and pause. Use that pause to translate the note into a single full idea, but don't say anything until that idea is firmly fixed in your mind. Once you've thought it through, express it at your normal rate of word delivery—which is generally as quickly as you can get the words out of your mouth.

After you've expressed the thought, let your audience absorb your idea. This is the second pause. It's the only point at which eye contact with the audience is necessary or desirable. In that pause, while glancing around, you're asking yourself: Do they understand? Are they ready for more? The audience needs time to think about each idea if they are going to participate in your presentation and relate your ideas to who they are as people.

Using good notes will help you explain ideas in the simplest possible terms. If you give your audience time to think, they'll take each simple idea and add their own level of sophistication. This helps them "participate" in the delivery of your information and allows them to personalize your ideas in a way that makes those ideas directly relevant to who they are as human beings.

Principle #9 — Think before you speak

In a conversation, you take time to form each thought before you say it. You should attempt to do the same thing at your presentations, although that can be much more difficult because of the impact of adrenaline.

Adrenaline is released into your system as a physiological response to stress—the stress of standing in front of the group. And adrenaline will have two effects on your ability to deliver your presentations.

First, it changes your time clock. It makes one second seem like eternity. The time you're taking to think through your ideas will seem like forever. As a result, you'll start talking before you're ready. But don't panic. Stop talking. Use your notes. Think through your next thought. Then start talking again. The pause always seems infinitely longer to you than it ever does to the audience.

Unfortunately, however, the second effect of adrenaline is that it inhibits your ability to think. In a stressful situation, adrenaline creates the fight-or-flight response, and there isn't much thinking involved with either option.

Questions are the best way to reduce nervousness.

This is also why I recommend that, wherever possible, you encourage questions throughout your presentations. Questions are the best way to reduce nervousness, as well as the stress and adrenaline your nervousness creates. As soon as the audience starts asking questions, the emphasis is taken off the formal presentation and moved toward having a more relaxed two-way conversation—safer ground for someone who's nervous. But keep your answers short.

Resist the pull of adrenaline. Stop talking. Think through each thought. Start talking again. Use good notes. Focus on delivering one idea at a time. This gets you off to a strong start. As for nervousness, never forget that the greatest reducer of nervousness in public speaking is a question or two that you can answer clearly, concisely, and confidently. At that point, presentations are turned into conversations.

Principle #10 — Silence is vital

There are two types of silence. One is for you to think before talking. This pause ends when you start talking. The second is the pause after you've expressed your thought, when you give the audience the opportunity to absorb what you just said.

During your presentations, remember that you're not there to prove you can talk non-stop. You're there to provide information for people to think about and apply to their personal circumstances. But remember, they can only think in silence, whether you provide that silence or they take it for themselves. Indeed, effective communicators use silence to influence when the audience thinks and what they think about.

If you lose your place or your audience, pause. If it's you who's lost, the pause allows you to think about where you are, where you're going, and what you need to say to get there. If your audience is lost, the pause will help them find their way back so they can listen to your ideas again and relate those ideas to their personal frame of reference.

Success in all conversations is relatively simple. The challenge is to use silence to influence when people think and what they think about.

The Key to Success

It's difficult to overstate the importance of understanding these principles and learning to apply them effectively during both your conversations and your presentations. But beyond that, they're equally applicable on both sides of the communication process. If you understand them, you can use them to enhance your listening skills.

For example, your audience can't think and listen at the same time, and neither can you. If you're thinking about what you're going to say to someone when they finally stop talking, you won't be able to hear or understand a word they're saying.

Listening is just as important as talking. In fact, the case could be made that it's even more important. There's an adage that tells us why human beings have two ears and only one mouth. In theory, we should spend twice as much time listening as we do talking.

If you learn to apply these principles to both sides of the communication process, both the listening side and the talking side, you will become a better communicator. By conversing instead of presenting, your communication effectiveness will improve, and this will have a positive effect on your results.

.

Step Five:
Answer Questions Throughout

For nearly twenty years, I have asked participants at my workshops, seminars and presentations whether we should encourage audience questions throughout our presentations, or save them until the end. There is no doubt that the majority of people opt for questions at the end when they deliver presentations.

"Why do you prefer that?" I ask.

"Because the presentation will get off track," they reply.

"But who gets off track?" I ask. "The person asking? Or the person answering?"

After a brief discussion, everyone soon realizes that the person answering usually gets off track. Their answers are long and convoluted. They often answer dozens of questions that weren't asked. Sometimes this is interesting to the audience. Most often it isn't.

What's amazing is how often we receive long and convoluted answers in our personal and professional lives. We all have a neighbor, friend, or family member who we're reluctant to ask "How are you today?" because it will be tomorrow or the next day before they get around to telling us how they were on what used to be today. These people don't wake up each day and think to themselves "How many people can I bore today?" They genuinely believe they're being social and/or helping other people to understand.

Long answers also occur
in professional situations—painfully so.

Long answers also occur in professional situations. In fact, painfully so—and often with negative outcomes. A few years ago, I was delivering a presentation to a group of consultants on the topic of communicating effectively during client pitches and sales presentations. The firm's CEO brought me in because he believed they weren't winning their share of business during shortlist presentations. When we discussed the skill of answering questions, I encouraged them to pause-answer-stop (pause, answer only the question that was asked, and stop talking). "But," countered one of the participants, "what if the question requires thirty minutes of explanation?"

I thought about that question then, and I've thought about it since. I would give the same answer now that I gave then. I don't believe there is a question on the planet that requires thirty minutes of answer. There certainly is not a question asked during a sales presentation that requires thirty minutes of answer. If you're even thinking of talking that much, you're not closing sales.

Our son's experience at university highlighted this for me. As a first-year business student, he was required to take calculus. At the start of the year, he told me during a Skype conversation that the professor was planning to devote two hours every second Friday morning to answering questions. Prior to attending the first question-and-answer (Q&A) class, our son prepared a list of questions he hoped to ask. We didn't talk about it again until he came home for a weekend about halfway through the semester.

"How have the Q&A classes in calculus been going?" I asked him.

"Not well, dad," he replied, looking a bit uncomfortable. "I only attended one class."

I must admit I had fleeting thoughts of tuition dollars flying out the window. But before going any further and negatively impacting my blood pressure, I asked: "Why only one?"

"Because it's the most boring two hours you could imagine," he said. "During the first class, the professor answered four questions."

If my math is correct, four questions in two hours equals approximately thirty minutes per answer. So much for thirty-minute answers. My son realized that he would be sleeping, whether in class or out, so he decided to exercise his rights as an adult and make it official. Every second Friday he slept in.

The vast majority of questions
can be answered in ten words or less.

There are mathematical problems that require thirty minutes of solution, but the person solving the problem should answer dozens of questions along the way. However, before ever turning to solve a problem, the professor should answer any "quick" questions at the start of class. As we'll explore during this chapter, the vast majority of questions can be answered in ten words or less. In fact, answering those questions early will likely enhance the learning process when mathematical problems are later solved for the group. The greater the number of questions the presenter answers per average minute of a presentation, the better the experience for everyone.

The next time you're answering questions, and you think your answer is too long, rest assured that it is. When any of us are answering questions about topics we're passionate about or on which we'd like to educate others, we're the last ones in the room to figure out that we've talked too much.

The purpose of this chapter is to provide you with insights you can apply to the challenge of answering questions effectively throughout your presentations, certainly, but also through every aspect of your personal and professional life. If you conscientiously implement the ideas in this chapter, your listening and communication skills will improve.

First, we're going to examine the ten-pushup rule. This is a training tool that never fails to improve listening skills. It also improves someone's ability to answer questions clearly, concisely, and effectively.

Next, we're going to examine the Q ratio, which is a simple measure of the number of questions asked and answered per unit of time. Quite simply, the higher your Q ratio, the better the communication process for everyone involved. Raising your Q ratio is easy. Keep your answers short.

Finally, we're going to examine what I call pause-answer-stop. When you're asked a question, take time to pause and think (which also supplements your listening skills), answer the question asked (and *only* the question asked), and then stop talking. This is the most difficult challenge imaginable in face-to-face communication, but the value it adds to the communication process is monumental. Hopefully, you'll retain pause-answer-stop and bring it to every question-and-answer challenge you experience throughout your personal and professional life.

The bottom line for answering questions is quite simple. If you want to take advantage of valuable opportunities to bring people together, questions need to be asked and answered along the way. On their own, people can read written documents, whether reports or presentation decks. When everyone gets together, those on the receiving end should have the opportunity to ask and explore, to probe further, and to relate specific aspects of the topic under discussion to their cognitive framework in a time-efficient process.

It doesn't matter whether someone is making decisions to write a feature article, launch a space shuttle, or manage risk at the boardroom table. More questions asked and answered by the receiver per minute leads to better decision making and, ultimately, better outcomes.

The Ten-Pushup Rule

As a training tool, I often introduce a slightly tongue-in-cheek guideline I call "the ten-pushup rule." The rule immediately underscores the value of succinct answers, but only one person has ever actually done the pushups—and then only because the volunteer was a particularly fit CEO.

The person answering gets
a maximum of ten words for the answer.

The rule is simple. The person answering the question gets a maximum of ten words for the answer. Any question. Ten words. We keep track. For every word over ten used, he or she will be required to do ten pushups per word at the end of the exchange.

This is an amazing tool. I've witnessed its positive impact thousands of times. When someone has a word limit on answers, his or her behavior immediately changes. First, the person answering begins to listen more carefully. This never ceases to amaze me. Think about it. When there's a limit on the length of the answer, people focus more attention on what's being asked. Their listening skills improve.

Second, the person answering the question communicates more effectively. He or she has no choice but to exactly and precisely meet the needs of the person asking. This puts the audience first in a two-way, receiver-driven exchange that also adheres to the principle of less is more. The question-and-answer process is the place where the presenter's knowledge meets the audience's need to understand. If handled properly, this is when communication can be most effective.

Third, the person answering the question doesn't have time to anticipate where questions are going. He or she deals with one question at a time. This prevents the person answering from making one of the biggest mistakes during the question-and-answer process: trying to anticipate where the person asking the questions is ultimately going.

My spouse and I have been together for more than twenty-five years. I cannot read her mind. Although she likes to think she can, she cannot read mine. If she's asking me a series of questions, I have discovered that attempting to anticipate where she's going is a tactic fraught with pitfalls and minefields. Providing long answers—in essence, trying to anticipate where questions are going—is very much like trying to read your spouse's mind. You might be right from time to time, but you'll be wrong more often than not.

If I can't read her mind, how can I anticipate questions on the mind of someone who I might have just met at my presentation? Even if I've heard the question thousands of times, it might be the first time the person asking has ever asked it. I try very hard to respect that by focusing on the question as if it's the first time I've heard it, and then answering succinctly.

Limiting the length of your answers will feel unnatural. Absolutely. But I often tell people they should learn to embrace that feeling. If you believe the answer was too short, it was probably perfect for whoever asked. If it was a complete answer, it probably seemed a bit long for those listening. If it was a full and complete answer, with just the right amount of important background information, guess what? No doubt, they all quit listening long ago.

I have evoked the ten-pushup
rule thousands of times.

I have evoked the ten-pushup rule thousands of times. It has never failed to improve someone's communication skills. One example, however, stands out in my mind as particularly striking, because it demonstrated the communication clarity that extremely short answers can facilitate.

I was providing a half-day of introductory media training for about a dozen senior managers of a municipality. With that big a group in a short time frame, there's not much opportunity to conduct practice media interviews. Near the end of the morning, however, I wanted to make the point that short answers are important to helping people understand.

So I made an unusual request. I asked for a volunteer, but with specific requirements: someone who probably lies or changes the subject if asked at a party what he or she does for a living. Everyone looked puzzled, so I clarified. I said I needed the one person in the room who, even though he or she has worked with others present for years, has a job no one really understands. At that point, everyone pointed to one person: the municipality's senior risk manager.

With some prompting from his peers, he came to the front of the room and sat down for his recorded interview. I began by asking him about his job and how he felt he added value to the municipality. During four minutes, I only managed to ask three or four questions. He wanted to educate me and the others about his job, especially since the group had clearly indicated they didn't currently understand what he did, so his answers were long. I let him talk.

At a certain point, I stopped him and asked how he thought he had done. "I think really well," he said. "I managed to get my points across." However, from his colleagues' expressions, I could tell they didn't understand any more now than they did before.

Then I evoked the ten-pushup rule. I told him we would keep track of the number of words he used per answer—we were recording, so it would be easy—and that for each word over ten, he would be asked to complete ten pushups per word at the end of the practice interview. I jokingly told him that he either learns to be brief or prepares to become fit.

I started the tape again and asked him about his job. The change in his demeanor was fascinating. He listened more carefully to what I was asking. He paused to think, simply answered the question, and then stopped talking.

At the end of two or three minutes, during which I asked about twenty-five questions, I stopped recording and thanked him for his participation. He got up, and all the way back to his seat, talked about how the second interview was terrible. He felt he didn't get a chance to tell me anything.

However, the reaction from the group made me smile. The best way to describe it is stunned silence. If it wasn't for the risk manager's grumbling on the way back to his seat, you could have heard a pin drop.

Short answers are significantly more effective.

When the manager sat down, the person beside him turned to him and said: "You and I have been close friends for five or six years, right? For the first time, I actually understand what you do for a living." I played the first and second interviews without interruption. When the risk manager watched and listened to the before and after versions, the look on his face showed that he clearly agreed.

Bottom line? Short answers are significantly more effective in helping people understand. Learn to self-evoke the ten-pushup rule with every presentation you deliver.

The Q Ratio

The Q ratio provides a simple measure of the relative interactivity of a presentation. Interactivity implies participation. Generally, the way audiences participate is to ask questions. In simplest terms, the Q ratio is the number of questions asked by the audience and answered by the presenter per minute for the length of the presentation. It applies only to questions asked by the audience. Any questions the presenter asks the audience are not included.

Wherever possible, strive for an absolute minimum Q ratio of one during your presentations. In other words, if you have a one-hour time frame, attempt to generate sixty-plus questions from the audience, which you answer clearly and concisely. If you deliver a thirty-minute presentation to introduce a new software program to a group of users, strive to answer at least thirty questions. If you deliver a one-hour presentation on market trends to prospects, encourage them to ask at least sixty questions. If you deliver a ninety-minute presentation to attendees at a conference, strive to answer ninety questions. And so on.

Is this achievable? Yes, it is. In fact, it's fairly easy to demonstrate that a Q ratio of one is a minimum standard. To demonstrate this, I often begin by asking the group to provide a time frame for the presentations they or others in their organization might deliver. Their answers vary from five minutes to a full day. Whenever possible, I get them to focus on one hour as the time frame for a presentation, including questions from the audience. I write this time frame down on a flip chart or whiteboard.

Next, I ask them to provide the maximum number of questions asked by the audience and answered by the presenter during presentations of that length, whether delivered by them or by others in their organization. Believe it or not, the most common response for questions from the audience during a one-hour presentation is four to five. That's four to five questions per hour of time the audience invests. This doesn't appear to be even remotely two-way, receiver-driven, or conversational.

The higher the Q ratio, the greater the interaction.

My thesis is simple. The higher the Q ratio, the greater the interaction between presenter and audience, or between sender and receiver in any interpersonal exchange. To demonstrate that a Q ratio of one is more than achievable, I often play a simple game called "do you drink coffee?"

To begin this exercise, I ask the group who they believe should control the direction of the question-and-answer process. The person asking? Or the person answering? Invariably, someone always picks answering. I then ask that person if he or she minds if I ask a few questions. Once I get permission to proceed, I ask a series of questions that often goes something like:

Do you drink coffee?

Yes

How many cups per day?

Two or three.

Always two or three?

Sometimes I might have more, but rarely.

Why would you drink more than three cups of coffee on a particular day?

I might have an afternoon meeting with a client over a cup of coffee.

Do you also drink coffee on weekends?

Yes.

If so, how many cups?

About the same.

How old were you when you started drinking coffee?

Fifteen or sixteen. Probably some time in high school.

Do you think high school is a little early to start drinking coffee?

No.

Did you drink coffee at university?

Yes.

What did you study at university?

I studied commerce.

I have played this game thousands of times. At this point, I stop and ask the group if they could have predicted that we were going to arrive at "What did you study at university?" from "Do you drink coffee?" None could. Then I ask if I could have predicted it. After a brief discussion, I hand my volunteer a piece of paper on which I've previously written "What did you study at university?" and ask them to read it aloud.

I have always been able to end at "What did you study at university?" from "Do you drink coffee?" within ten to twelve questions, generally in a minute or less. Ten questions in one minute equals a Q ratio of ten.

At this point, I return to the flip chart on which I write "60" as the time frame for the group's presentations, make some assumptions, and do some simple algebra. The "60" represents the time frame of a potential presentation. If communication is a two-way process, half that time belongs to the audience. It's their chance to participate, explore, and ask. If I can ask ten questions in one minute, the audience has the potential to ask x questions in thirty minutes.

The math is:

10 questions in one minute

x questions in 30 minutes

$x = 30 \times 10 = 300$ questions

Potentially, if the answers are kept to ten words or less, a presenter could answer three hundred questions in a sixty-minute time frame, for a Q ratio of five. Will you ever get there? Probably not. However, it is possible to achieve a Q ratio of more than one in almost every circumstance, every presentation, and certainly every one-on-one interaction with other human beings. Answering four or five questions in sixty minutes is not even remotely good enough.

Highlights Number of Points

The "Do you drink coffee?" exchange highlights a number of key points. First, it establishes who determines the direction of the question-and-answer process. Should the person answering determine the direction? Or should the person asking questions steer the exchange? My philosophy is simple. The person asking questions should be in charge if the intent is to follow the path of clear communication that leads to improved decision making and win-win outcomes. This is two-way, receiver-driven, and conversational.

The "Do you drink coffee?" exercise also demonstrates how many questions can be asked and answered in a short period of time. It usually takes about a minute to ask ten to fifteen questions in a way that makes each question a natural extension of the one before. It leads to a Q ratio of ten or higher.

To demonstrate the difference between short and long answers, I often repeat the person's answers back to the group with something like: "I'm glad you asked that question. Yes, as a matter of fact, I do drink coffee. Normally I drink two to three cups a day. Sometimes I might have more, but rarely. I might have an afternoon meeting with a client over a cup of coffee. I also drink coffee on weekends. Again, it's about two to three cups.

"I started drinking coffee when I was about fifteen or sixteen years of age. It was sometime in high school. I don't think high school was too early to start drinking coffee. I drank coffee at university. I studied commerce at university, and it was a wonderful foundation on which I've constructed my career."

*We have to ask ourselves if this is
how questions are usually answered.*

People usually have a good laugh when information is presented back to them in this way. But when the laughter dies down, we have to ask ourselves if this is how questions are usually answered during presentations, staff meetings, board meetings, sales presentations, media interviews, and all kinds of other one-on-one exchanges within our personal and professional lives. Most of us genuinely want to help other people understand, so our natural instinct when asked questions is to give more information, not less. But we need to learn that the best way to help people understand anything is to shorten answers and increase the Q ratio. Less is always more.

Objections to Answering Questions

There are a number of objections to answering questions from start to finish during presentations. People often say that the topic dictates whether questions should be answered throughout or left to the end. Quite honestly, I don't think the topic matters at all. By asking questions, the audience can better understand my content or yours—any content—so they can either apply that content or act on it.

Granted, if a relatively simple concept is explained during a five-minute update at a regular team meeting, people may not need to ask many questions to improve their understanding. However, if the concept is even remotely complex, people need to ask. You can't simply march through your information and expect it to magically generate understanding at the end.

Let's suppose someone asks a question about an issue you plan to cover later in the presentation. What do you do? Many people don't answer the question when it's asked, politely directing the person to hold onto the question until the presentation gets to that topic area.

However, if we examine this approach from the perspective of the principles in *Step Four*, is it two-way? Is it receiver-driven? One could make the case that it adheres to the principle of less is more. But consider the ability of a person to listen and think at the same time. Is it possible? No, it is not. If you ask the person to hold onto a question, he or she will consider it as a request *de facto* to keep thinking about that question until you choose to answer it. Thus, you're essentially asking them to stop listening.

Answer the question succinctly.

When you're asked a question, even on a subject you're going to cover later, self-evoke the ten-pushup rule and answer the question succinctly. If the person has follow-up questions, answer those succinctly as well. Keeping answers short meets individual needs and can take very little time. When you cover the topic later, your content will simply reinforce your earlier answers.

Some people are happy answering questions one-on-one over lunch, but resist when the audience gets even marginally larger (i.e. a group of ten or twelve). Yes, audience size can have an impact. However, with audiences of fifty participants or fewer, questions should always be handled throughout. There is no reasonable excuse for not doing so. Members of the group can be heard when they ask questions. The presenter can be heard when he or she answers. Ergo, the group has an open exchange from start to finish.

With larger groups, microphones can be strategically placed throughout the room. They can either be set on stands, or two or three people with cordless microphones can circulate throughout the room. With a group of virtually any size, questions can be effectively incorporated and answered throughout your presentations.

By asking numerous questions, audiences large and small can probe the specific areas of your knowledge important to their need to understand. This is something you can never predict; it is something only they can determine with certainty. This enables them to make informed and effective decisions—to either apply the information you're presenting or take action on it.

Pause-Answer-Stop

The most important skill we can hone to communicate effectively is the ability to answer questions clearly and concisely through pause-answer-stop. Our friends will thank us. Our families will thank us. Our colleagues will thank us. Our staff will thank us. Our bosses and clients will thank us. And whenever we deliver presentations, our audiences will thank us.

This simple concept enables us to communicate effectively. The reason? The people receiving information get to ask questions directly related to their need to understand, which is something we can never predict. People can teach themselves at a pace appropriate for them. If we believe they are the most important people in the room, that pace needs to be respected and honored. Answer questions from start to finish wherever and whenever possible.

A few years ago, my wife and I decided to put ceramic tile through our entranceway and kitchen. We were undecided about whether to do the job ourselves or hire a contractor.

One evening, I went to our local Home Depot to do some research. I had the good fortune of encountering a very confident young man who had obviously installed a lot of ceramic tile. How did I know he was confident? He didn't feel compelled to talk endlessly whenever I asked him a question. In fact, he simply answered each question and stopped talking, waiting patiently for the next question to be asked.

In the fifteen or twenty minutes that we chatted, I easily asked more than one hundred questions. Our daughter was with me, and as we were walking out of the store she remarked: "Dad, that was amazing. I can't believe how much I learned. Even I know what needs to be done to install tiles. You asked great questions."

I was simply given the opportunity to ask a lot of questions.

Actually, I didn't ask great questions. I was simply given the opportunity to ask a lot of questions—which never would have happened if the person answering hadn't simply paused, answered the question, and stopped talking.

Short answers improve decision-making at all levels. I recently had a frustrating experience with my dentist. She informed me that I have some bone loss and may need to visit a periodontist. To say I was concerned is an understatement. I can easily count on one hand the number of days I have not flossed my teeth during the past ten years.

After she informed me of this issue, a number of questions immediately came to mind. When I finally managed to ask a question (basically when she stopped to take a breath), I was greeted with another barrage of information, yet the answer to the question was nowhere to be found.

A number of times, I could see from her expression that she could see from my expression that I had more questions to ask which I believed were important. But she kept talking, even raising her voice slightly, and speaking more quickly to make her point.

There are a number of issues that could be examined here, but let's focus on the receiver's perspective and the principles discussed during the last chapter. As the receiver of information, the question I'd like to ask is important to me. To make sure I don't forget the question, I bring it from long-term memory to working memory. While working memory is filled with that question, it can't process new information. I can't listen to what the person is saying. You might as well stop when you see that someone has a question. There is absolutely no value to saying another word.

Now, let me be clear. I love our dentist. She has looked after my entire family for nearly twenty years. But when I got home and told my wife, I was unable to answer the most basic question she asked: "Where in your mouth is it? Everywhere? Or is it in a couple of places?"

My experience with my dentist reminded me of an exchange I had with an emergency physician while speaking at a conference. She was challenging my assertion that pause-answer-stop is preferable. "If a patient's spouse asks if their partner is in danger of dying," she said, "we can't just answer yes or no. We have to give longer answers to help them understand. We have to provide comfort."

One of those two words—yes or no—
is the first thing I want to hear.

If it was my spouse under discussion, one of those two words—yes or no—is the first thing I want to hear when I ask if she's in danger of dying. Truthfully, either yes or no would be the *only* thing I want to hear. Regardless of whether the answer is yes or no, my thought processes will go into overdrive, driven by relief on one hand or potential concern on the other. If it's bad news, my thoughts will immediately turn to our family. Should I contact them? How will I contact them? Where are they? What do I tell them?

I won't hear a word the physician is saying until I decide what questions need to be asked and answered first, so I can make decisions. If the family has not yet been informed of an accident or incident, my need for information will be different than if they already know. How critical is this? Should they stay home? Or would this be the last opportunity to say good-bye?

As I sort through this series of possible actions and outcomes, I will have questions. I will soon be ready to re-engage with the physician, but not to listen. My priority will be to ask first, then listen. When I listen, I will be only listening for the specific answer to my questions. Filler words before each answer will frustrate me. Filler words after the answer will be lost, because I'll already be thinking about my next question. The best comfort the physician can provide is to clearly and concisely answer any and all questions I have. More questions asked and answered per unit of time—a higher Q ratio—improves decision making. Period.

Pause Before Responding

Regardless of whether you're answering questions during group presentations or one-on-one, there are a number of distinct advantages to pausing before answering. First, it's polite. If you have someone in your life who starts answering the question before you've finished asking, you know how rude this can be. Pausing allows you to provide short answers without seeming rude or abrupt. If you shoot back a yes or no without pausing, you create a completely different perception than if you pause, consider the question and respond with "yes" or "no."

Second, you can think during the pause. Thinking before talking is always good. You can ensure you understand the question, so you can provide the best possible answer, which is almost always the shortest possible answer.

You look confident when you pause. People in control of themselves and their environment take time to compose their response. Contrast this with those who blurt out answers. If you've ever conducted a job interview with someone young and inexperienced, you know exactly what I'm talking about.

By pausing, you compliment the questioner. You actually say "that was a good question" without ever opening your mouth. The question required time to think, therefore it was a good question. This brings us to another point. You cannot buy time to think by telling someone that they asked a good question. If you need time to think (and we almost always do!), take it. In silence.

Pausing before answering enables you to control emotion.

Pausing before answering enables you to control emotion during stressful exchanges. If you're ever participated in a question-and-answer exchange where emotions run high, you likely know the value of pausing, or the risks associated with not pausing. By pausing, you can influence the pace at which questions are asked. Generally, people will allow you to answer one question before asking you another.

There are situations where you might get asked a number of questions at once. For example, someone might ask: "Are you sure you should keep your answers short? What if the answer requires a lengthy answer? What if people want to know more?" By pausing, you can sort through these multiple questions before trying to answer them. Confirm each question before answering. You might respond by saying: "Let me see if I understand your questions. Should we always keep our answer short? Absolutely. What if the question requires a lengthy answer? Most questions can be answered in ten words or less. If people want to know more, they'll ask more questions."

Pausing can help establish a pattern that makes difficult questions seem less obvious. If someone asks a series of questions that you answer quickly, difficult questions become obvious because it's the first time you pause. If you've established a pattern of pausing throughout, that difficult question is not as obvious. This provides you with a level of protection.

Finally, you become a better listener by pausing. As we discussed during the last chapter, human beings cannot think and listen at the same time. So if you feel the need to answer the question as soon as it's asked, you're already thinking about the answer while the person is still asking. Establishing a pattern of pausing before answering enables you to separate listening and thinking, which then enhances your listening skills.

How long should you pause? It depends, but generally as long as you need to match the correct answer to the question asked. Pause at least a second or so to ensure that you're polite and complimentary and to prevent difficult questions from standing out. However, if you need more time to think, take it. If you start talking before you're ready, two things will happen. First, your answers will be longer because you're still thinking while talking. Second, they will also be less precise and ultimately less communicative.

Be careful with loaded questions, or questions that are asked on the basis of an incorrect assumption. For example, suppose someone asks: "You've said this software platform will not be ready on time, so how critical is it that we get you the information by next Friday?" If the initial premise of this question is incorrect, you must remove it or clarify the misperception before answering. A possible reply could be: "I didn't say the software won't be ready on time. We're currently a bit behind schedule. Getting information by Friday will put us back on schedule."

Repeating a question to buy yourself time to think doesn't work.

Repeating a question when the audience has difficulty hearing is polite. Repeating a question to buy yourself time to think doesn't work. However, if you're unsure what someone is asking, don't guess. Check with them. Rephrase the question and ask: "Was that what you were asking?" Once you get confirmation that it was, pause to form an appropriate answer.

The skill of answering questions is the art of matching the clear, concise answer directly to the question asked. This should be your focus. Don't try to predict where the questions are going. After all, how can you reasonably predict what someone else is thinking? My spouse and I have been together for a long time and each of us knows the range of behaviors that will please or upset the other, but even these can change on a moment's notice. Neither of us can read the other's mind.

Whenever an answer extends for more than ten seconds, you're already making assumptions about what's important to whoever asked the question. Virtually every question ever asked can be answered in ten seconds or less. Truthfully, the vast majority of those can be answered in ten words or less.

While pausing, always resist the temptation to create a decision tree in your head when someone asks a question. In other words, don't engage in a mental exercise of: "If I answer this, he or she will ask that. Then if I answer that ..."

When you create a decision tree, answers become imprecise. They're longer. They're widely open to interpretation, so they're often interpreted along a wide spectrum. People don't remember what you say. They remember what they thought about what you said, and at the end of the exchange they'll have differing viewpoints about what was said. This is counterproductive if your goal is to update, educate, inform, persuade, sell, or facilitate effective decision making. Precise, succinct answers support every one of these goals. Of course, if your goal is to obfuscate, then by all means pontificate.

Answer the Question Asked

At the core, people who ask a question are seeking one thing: *the* answer. They're not seeking another speech or presentation. They're rarely seeking more than the smallest amount of additional information. They're generally not seeking answers to questions yet unasked. They're simply seeking the answer to the question asked.

In your daily life, when people ask, "What time is it?" you don't tell them you're glad they asked that question or say "that's a good question." You don't provide them with background information related to your watch, then go into a lengthy description of that background. You simply look at your watch and answer the question.

If the answer is "yes," people will want to hear it. And the same applies if the answer is "no," "possibly," "absolutely," "eventually," "unlikely," or "only under specific conditions." How much more they want or need to hear will surprise you when you begin examining the question-and-answer process from the perspective of the concepts discussed here. As a general statement, questioners almost always want less than the person answering feels compelled to provide.

If the answer to the question is "under certain circumstances," tell them so and stop. If they're interested in the circumstances, they'll ask. If not, move on. Trust me. If people believe that answering their questions is important to you and your answers are succinct, they'll ask more questions if they're remotely interested.

If answers are lengthy, audiences simply stop asking questions.

However, if answers are lengthy, audiences simply stop asking questions. I've witnessed this hundreds of times at presentations I've attended, but one of the more amusing examples occurred a number of years ago when I was providing presentation training to rookie advisors at a brokerage firm. My program was embedded as part of their training. Even though these advisors might never deliver group presentations as part of their business development, the vice-president of training understood the value of teaching a conversational approach to communicating effectively in all situations, including one-on-one. He also believed that advisors needed to answer questions effectively, so we put particular emphasis on the Q&A process.

Each class was scheduled for an evening and subsequent full day. My normal habit was to arrive for the catered dinner, then conduct the evening session from 6:30 to 8:30 p.m. On one occasion, I arrived an hour early, so I decided to watch the consultant ahead of me.

With about ten minutes remaining before the dinner break, one of the participants asked a closed question that technically required a "yes" or "no" answer. The consultant told the group he was going to give them the short answer, so I thought I'd time him. I started my watch. Fourteen minutes later, he stopped for a breath and asked: "Are there any more questions?"

While he was going through his answer, the catering company delivered dinner just outside the training room door. The door was closed, but the odors were wafting through to tease us. My stomach was growling long before he completed his answer. Prior to that, however, the person who asked the question put his feet up on the desk to read the newspaper, with the newspaper between him and the person answering. Almost everyone else was checking e-mail at the terminals in front of them. Not a soul was listening. When he finally stopped to ask if there were any additional questions, everyone immediately stopped what they were doing and started glancing around the room. The message they were sending each other was clear, if unspoken: "Don't you dare ask another question."

Short answers are counter intuitive. Most of us feel that providing short answers either shortchanges the person asking or makes us look as if we are not knowledgeable about our subject area.

A number of years ago, during presentation training, one of the participants told me his clients would not take him seriously if he didn't provide full and complete answers to their questions. His clients are members of pension committees with a wide range of investment knowledge. He's a fixed-income manager. "My clients need to know that I know what I'm talking about," he said. "It's also my job to educate them about the investment process wherever possible."

No problem, I thought to myself. When this person later delivered a presentation, I asked what I thought was a relatively straightforward question: "Given the fact you say you don't make bets on portfolio duration, isn't the way you work the yield curve similar to a bet on duration?"

Technically, this is a closed question that simply requires a "yes" or "no." For him, the correct answer was "no." His focus on the yield curve has nothing to do with portfolio duration. However, he went on for more than four minutes before I interrupted him to ask another question.

The exchange was video recorded. When I played back the recording, we watched all four minutes uninterrupted. When I stopped the recording, I said: "Unlike most of your clients, I can calculate duration within a bond portfolio, yet I am completely confused by your answer and don't have a clue what you're talking about right now."

He looked quite sheepish and responded with: "If you could understand what I'm talking about, I'd be really impressed. I'm watching me and I don't have a clue what I'm saying." Later, he told me that watching the playback was the longest four minutes of his life.

You can practice this skill
every day of your life.

The beauty of the skill of answering questions is that you can practice every day of your life, whether in personal or professional settings. We all answer questions every day. In your daily life, I recommend that you teach yourself the invaluable skill of answering questions directly and succinctly. Even if it's a "tough" question (i.e. one that challenges you directly or touches a sensitive area of your personal or professional life), you should still answer it concisely. If you ignore it, if you evade or waffle in any way, the audience will certainly notice, and your credibility will be affected. If you go on too long, they'll often stop listening. And more often than not they'll simply stop asking questions.

There are three acceptable answers to every question you can be asked, whether you're asked one-on-one or during a group presentation:

- Yes, I have the answer, and here it is.

- No, I don't have the answer, but I'll get it for you.

- Yes, I do have the answer, but I cannot provide it to you.

There are very specific cases in which you would use the third response—for example, if providing the answer would divulge sensitive competitive information or break client confidentiality. In every other case, the first two answers apply. Either you have the answer and you'll provide it, or you don't have it and you'll get it.

Stop Talking

After you answer each question, stop talking. This is the hardest challenge of face-to-face communication, whether one-on-one or with groups. However, the value it brings to the communication process is impossible to overstate. If the audience wants more, they'll ask, especially if you create a two-way, interactive exchange in which they feel comfortable asking questions.

If your answers are short, you can better adhere to the principles we discussed during *Step Four*. Shorter answers create a better two-way exchange. They're receiver-driven, because receivers get the opportunity to have their needs met. They support the principle of less is more; the less you say, the more they actually understand. This adds tremendous value.

If you're unsure of what is being asked, stop and clarify. If you feel you've answered the question, stop. If you see a puzzled expression, stop. If you see that the other person has a question, stop. When in doubt, stop. Clarify. Answer. Let them teach themselves by creating a two-way, receiver-driven exchange that improves communication and enhances decision making.

During a luncheon conversation on the first day of a two-day training program, a client and I were talking about the baseball team I coached as a volunteer when he suddenly asked me how to pitch a curve ball. This is a subject I'm passionate about. I could have talked all day about curve balls, including that I've always been reluctant to teach the pitch to young players to protect their arms. But I didn't for two reasons. First, I like to practice what I preach; I genuinely wanted him to understand. Second, he had been a bit skeptical of my advice around short answers, so I thought this might be a good test for both of us.

I kept my answers short and let him steer the conversation. He asked about spin and direction, then how dramatically the ball can curve during the short distance from pitcher's mound to home plate. He asked why and when such a pitch should be thrown. In time, he began asking about pitch count strategy. During fifteen or twenty minutes, he easily asked more than a hundred questions.

The next day at lunch, he sought me out. "I watched a baseball game last night," he told me. "For the first time, I enjoyed it. I've always thought it's a boring game, and now I realize it isn't. But I have a few more questions."

After a few minutes, he suddenly stopped and gave me a strange look. "You're doing it to me, aren't you?" he asked.

"Doing what?" I responded.

"You're keeping your answers short to make your point," he challenged.

"Am I keeping my answers short? Absolutely. Am I doing so to make a point? Not really. I'm keeping my answers short because I'm really enjoying how you're teaching yourself about a subject that I'm quite passionate about."

True Value of Communication

The true value of communication is its role in enabling senders and receivers to create a back-and-forth exchange that results in a shared reality. By reading this book, you began the process when you put audience needs first. The question-and-answer process is the finishing touch. By encouraging audience questions throughout your presentations, you create a better exchange of ideas to create win-win outcomes with your audiences in support of your business and communication objectives.

> *The greater the level of engagement, the better the exchange.*

Logically, the greater the level of engagement, the better the exchange of information and ideas. Let's suppose you attend two presentations as an audience member. During the first, the audience asks four or five questions at the end of a half-hour presentation. During the second, you and other members of the audience ask thirty or more questions throughout the presentation. Everything being equal, which presentation is more engaging? Which one creates a better communication environment? Which one forms a stronger foundation on which a shared reality can be constructed?

To achieve higher levels of engagement, learn to self-evoke the ten-pushup rule during your presentations, certainly, but also attempt to self-evoke it during conversations of all kinds. Keep your answers focused and succinct. Trust me. Your friends, family, and colleagues will appreciate your efforts.

Strive for a Q ratio of one or more as a minimum standard during all presentations. From start to finish during your presentations, ask people: "Are there any questions?" After you ask, scan the group. Make eye contact. Pause. If you follow this process a number of times, it doesn't take long before they start asking. Over time and with practice, you should consistently achieve Q ratios higher than one.

This is only achievable, however, if you follow pause-answer-stop. The most important point here is to match the answer to the question asked. Think about the question. Say your answer. Stop talking. If you can do that, you'll discover an added benefit: your listening skills will improve.

I started my communication career in the dark ages of the information age, when phototypesetting was state-of-the-art. Phototypesetting is a now-outdated technology that bridged the gap between pouring hot lead to set type and what became known as desktop publishing.

During the past thirty-plus years, as my career has evolved in the information age, I have discovered two truths about communication. First, it's infinitely more valuable to communicate than it is to transmit. Second, within the communication process itself, it is infinitely more valuable to listen than it is to talk.

As a society, I believe we will mature in the information age only when we embrace those two truths, both individually and in groups. Listen before you talk. And when you talk, don't transmit. Communicate.

Overcoming the Addiction

The PowerPoint phenomenon has become a surreal form of behavioral social addiction, complete with enabling behavior. An addiction can be viewed as a continued involvement with a substance or activity despite the negative consequences associated with it.[xix] Are there negative consequences? Yes there are, and they are starting to be well documented.

A *New York Times* article talks about the use of PowerPoint in the military. "PowerPoint makes us stupid," one general is quoted as saying. The military decision makers on the receiving end of slides complain about stifled discussion and a lack of critical thinking. They also worry about the effect on thoughtful decision-making.[xx] If PowerPoint's impact on intelligence and critical thinking is that bad, then there are deadly consequences, especially in a theater of war. It makes you wonder why those at the front lines keep feeding PowerPoint to their commanders. If it were me, I'd look for a better way. I wouldn't want critical thinking or decision-making to be negatively impacted, particularly when my life or my friends' lives might depend on it.

Like any addiction, PowerPoint is difficult to stop.

The addiction and subsequent negative consequences are evident in classrooms, conference halls, training rooms, and boardrooms—virtually everywhere. Like any addiction, PowerPoint is difficult to stop, even when there is absolutely no reason to continue. If you've ever been addicted to cigarettes, alcohol, drugs, sex, food, exercise, or anything else, you know you can't think of life without that substance.

Think it's easy to break the habit? Imagine this scenario: You have a job interview next week. It's your second interview and you've been told that you have to develop a 10-minute presentation for delivery to the selection committee on your vision for this job. You can bring notes to your presentation, and you have the choice of sitting or standing when you deliver, but you can't show a single slide. There's no projector in the room and the interview panel has all the information about you they need, so they don't want a handout of any type. No laptop. No printed presentation deck. If you hadn't read this book, how would you prepare if faced with such a challenge? Interesting thought, isn't it?

The *New York Times* article points out that one general has expressed a dim view of briefings via decks. The implication is that everyone reporting to him knows it, yet "a third of his briefings are [delivered] by PowerPoint."[xxi] In other words, about a third of the people who present to this particular general are risking double negative consequences. Not only has one commander in the Middle East publicly stated that bullet points make him stupid, their specific commander doesn't want his briefings delivered via PowerPoint, but a third of his junior officers bring PowerPoint anyway.

We now find ourselves with both an addiction and an enabling behavior. The receiver of the information—in this case, the general—bears responsibility because he is also negatively impacted. This is why he expressed a dim view of PowerPoint in the first place. Neither the senders of information (junior officers using PowerPoint) nor the receiver (the general who dislikes PowerPoint but puts up with it) seem willing or able to stop, yet in theory it should be relatively easy to do.

I have never had the privilege of serving in the armed forces, but I have a very good friend who was an officer in the US Navy. We worked together on an international volunteer committee for a professional association that he joined shortly after retiring from active service.

He told me civilian life took a bit of adjustment. It took some time to get used to the fact that sailors didn't snap to attention when he entered a room. As I read the *New York Times* article, I couldn't help but think that the general could easily solve his problem by ordering that PowerPoint not be used during briefings. In theory, nobody would disobey a direct order.

But he didn't issue that order, thereby becoming an enabler of this surreal addiction. And here we are, both sides with negative consequences. One doesn't want to bore the other. The other doesn't want to be bored. One wants to help the other make effective decisions. The other wants to make decisions effectively. Both know that PowerPoint isn't helping, but neither knows what else to do.

Stop Enabling the Behavior

During the year it took to write this book, I talked to dozens upon dozens of people about it. They represented a wide range of industries, expertise, and interests—from senior executives to freelance entrepreneurs, from communication professionals to engineers, lawyers, doctors, dentists, financial analysts, economists, not-for-profit professionals, and more. Their most common response was: "I can't wait until the book comes out. I'm tired of having to sit through all those PowerPoint presentations."

The first six chapters of this book are devoted to those who develop and deliver presentations. With luck, the first chapter helped them realize that there is no sound basis for which to continue blindly creating presentations on slideware programs—whether they're using PowerPoint, Keynote, Prezi, SlideRocket, or any program yet to be invented. 'Death by PowerPoint' is created when a slideware program is used to create the presentation. Boredom and lost productivity are merely symptoms. The true demon is the flawed critical thinking process that occurs by pointing, clicking, typing, and then attempting to present the finished product. This behavior needs to be avoided at all costs.

The five steps are designed
to provide a reasonable solution.

The second-most common response I received when someone learned about this book was, "What's the alternative?" We're now at the point where millions of people around the world cannot conceive of developing and/or delivering a presentation without PowerPoint. Thus, the five steps are designed to provide a reasonable solution by which presentations can be developed and delivered with best practices of communication effectiveness in mind. If presenters put their audiences first, structure conversations (not presentations), minimize visual aids, convey their message and personality, and answer questions throughout, their ability to communicate will improve. And so will their results.

This chapter is devoted to everyone else—those of us who sit through presentations developed and delivered by others. The following Audience Manifesto™ is designed to provide all of us with a simple tool by which we can politely say "Enough is enough." With that in mind, if you truly believe that enough is enough, I encourage you to communicate the following:

Thank you for agreeing to deliver a presentation to us. We're looking forward to a meaningful exchange of ideas. We hope you'll keep the following in mind:

Please put our needs first
We know you have knowledge and insights to share. If you didn't, you wouldn't be here. However, please tailor your knowledge to our specific needs, so we can both gain from our time together.

Please structure a conversation
We prefer a conversation, not a presentation. We appreciate ideas being put into context; we have no desire to participate in a "data dump."

Please minimize your visual aids
Every visual you use must add value. And don't be afraid to use a variety of tools—whiteboards, appropriate props, YouTube videos, or a piece of paper, if necessary. If you sent a handout in advance, please assume that we've read it. We have no desire to walk through it again.

Please facilitate a conversation
We are looking forward to a two-way exchange, in which ideas are shared, not transmitted.

Please answer questions
Allow us to put your information into context by asking questions. But please keep your answers as brief as possible, so we can ask more questions during our time together.

A stylized .pdf poster of this manifesto can be downloaded at www. FiveStepsToConquer.html/manifesto.html. Technically, someone doesn't even need to read this book to improve their presentations by keeping in mind the five points above. In theory, they can be sent in advance to presenters and/or posted wherever presentations are delivered:

- If you're in charge of training and development for your organization, you could send a copy of the poster or an e-mail of it to your internal training resources and/or your external suppliers.

- If you chair a board of directors, and assuming you haven't banned projected PowerPoint at your meetings (which is something I strongly encourage), you could make this poster available in the waiting room outside your boardroom and have a laminated copy affixed to the spot at which presentations to your board are delivered.

- If you're organizing a conference, you could send these points to presenters in advance. Your attendees will thank you. You could also include these points in presenter evaluations as part of the standard you expect.

- If you're a member of your organization's senior management team, encouraging the adoption of these concepts during presentations you view will save you time and enhance your decision making.

- If you receive short-list presentations from suppliers—whether advertising agencies, PR agencies, insurance providers, leasing companies, consultants, investment managers or others—send a copy of these points to everyone on the shortlist. Reward those who follow them during their presentations.

- If you're a student at college or university, and your professors are overusing slides, discretely leave a copy of these points on their desks— and keep doing so until they get the message. Your education is far too expensive to have its effectiveness negatively impacted by slides, especially when there is no direct evidence to support the assumption that slides are remotely effective in the classroom. Any classroom.

It's OK to Not Use PowerPoint

During my introductory French course, our oral examination was to develop and deliver a twenty-sentence presentation in French. As you can imagine, some people opted for PowerPoint. As the class progressed, those who hadn't prepared PowerPoint slides for their presentation began apologizing for not doing so when they got to the front of the room.

My presentation was in the middle of the evening's proceedings. When I stood up, I asked the instructor for permission to say something briefly in English before switching to French. "No problem," was her reply.

I informed my classmates that I was writing a book entitled *Five Steps to Conquer 'Death by PowerPoint'*. "Je n'aime pas le PowerPoint," I said, "I do not like PowerPoint." This left little doubt in anyone's mind where I stood, "so could we please stop apologizing for not bringing it?"

There was not a single apology for the remainder of the evening. I made an interesting observation that night. Once the expectation of bringing PowerPoint is removed, people seem to just relax and focus on communicating effectively.

So if there are any lingering doubts, let me put them to rest. Focus on the audience's needs. Be prepared. Create a two-way exchange. Encourage and answer questions throughout. Engage their minds and, chances are, the audience won't notice if you don't use a single slide.

My Hope for the Future

My wish for presentations of the future is that, as audience members, we'll be comfortable letting presenters know that we would like to receive information that meets our need to understand. We want value from that information, the why and the how of it. Why is this important to us? How will this help us?

I hope we'll be comfortable letting presenters know that we want them to understand us—not only who we are on the outside, but our beliefs, attitudes, and opinions. We want the presentation to be tailored to our specific needs. If they are well prepared, we absolutely do not care if they don't use a single slide. If they use slides, they will only do so if every single one adds value.

In the future, I hope we'll be comfortable with presenters who get to the point. We will want to know how we should apply the information or take action on it. We will want to know this early in the process, preferably right up front. This will help us relate their information to our personal cognitive framework. This is when communication works.

My wish is that we will want presenters to understand that we do not attend presentations thinking: "I hope the slides are entertaining," or "I wonder which seductive font the presenter will use." If written information is needed to move ideas along, we'll want to see it in advance. If more detailed information is needed later, we'll want it later, not during the presentation. I hope we'll have the courage to stop presenters who ignore this wish. During precious "face time," we want information put into perspective. We do not want data driven down our throats.

If we can work together to bring about this end state, this wish for the future, we really will change the world, one conversation at a time.

Endnotes

i   Sweller, John, "Visualisation and Instructional Design," School of Education, University of New South Wales, Sydney, Australia, April 2007.

ii   Bumiller, Elizabeth, "We Have Met the Enemy and He Is PowerPoint," *New York Times*, April 26, 2010.

iii   Lane, Robert & Vlcek, Andre, *Selling Visually With PowerPoint*, Aspire Communications, 2009, page 371.

iv   Grunig, James, *Excellence in Public Relations and Communication Management*, Lawrence Erlbaum Associates, 1992, page 19.

v   Grunig, page 307.

vi   Gallo, Carmine, *The Presentation Secrets of Steve Jobs*, McGraw Hill, 2010, page 3.

vii   Lerner, Kevin, "How to create a great presentation in under four hours," as shown at www.squidoo.com/four-hour-presentation.

viii   Bonner, Allan, *Bonner's Lemon Law*, YouTube, Feb 1, 2007, www.youtube.com/user/AllanBonner#p/search/2/q-jxY2o35Wo.

viv   James, Geoffrey, Avoiding "Death by PowerPoint," as shown at http://www.bnet.com/blog/salesmachine/avoiding-death-by-powerpoint/10.

x   Dorothy D. Billington, Seven Characteristics of Highly Effective Adult Learning Programs, New Horizons for Learning, Seattle, WA, as provided at www.newhorizonsorg.

xi   Mehrabian, p. 56.

xii   Edberg, Henrik, "18 ways to improve your body language," *Positivity Blog*, as shown at http://www.positivityblog.com/index.php/2006/10/27/18-ways-to-improve-your-body-language.

xiii   Urs Bender, Peter, *Secrets of PowerPresentations*, The Achievement Group, Toronto, Canada, 1991, page 101.

xiv   Morgan, Nick, "How to Become an Authentic Speaker," *Harvard Business Review*, November 2008, page 1.

xv   Wikipedia.

xvi   Goldin-Meadow, Susan, *Hearing Gesture: How Our Hands Help Us Think*, Harvard University Press, Cambridge, MA, 2003, page 3.

xvii   Goldin-Meadow, page 180.

xviii   Begley, Sharon, *Wall Street Journal*, as reproduced in the *Chicago Sun-Times*, November 25, 2003, page 14.

xix   Source: Wikipedia. As cited: Dan J. Stein; Eric Hollander; Barbara Olasov Rothbaum (31 August 2009). Textbook of Anxiety Disorders. American Psychiatric Pub. pp. 359.

xx   Bumiller, Elizabeth, "We Have Met the Enemy and He Is PowerPoint," *New York Times*, April 26, 2010.

xxi   Ibid.

About the Author

Eric Bergman has never been, nor will he ever become, a fan of any slide-ware program that is even remotely overused. He has felt this way for a long time. He was "overdosed on overheads" at an early age. And, as someone who has found creative ways to avoid 'Death by PowerPoint' throughout his career, he has no desire to be Killed by Keynote or Pummeled by Prezi.

He believes that the spoken word and the written word must be separate to be effective. Simply put, audiences can read or they can listen, but they cannot read and listen at the same time.

"This is actually quite easy to demonstrate," he says. "The next time you're watching your favorite all-news channel, try listening to what's being said while reading what's scrolling across the bottom. It shouldn't take longer than ten seconds to prove the point."

He believes smart presenters tap into this principle, and others, to improve their success. He believes this book and the free downloadable workbook at www.FiveStepsToConquer.com will show them how.

For the past 30 years, Eric Bergman's approach has helped countless professionals from five continents become better communicators—from C-Suite executives to front-line supervisors and everything in between. If you're interested in booking Eric as a speaker, or providing training to those in your organization, please visit www.FiveStepsToConquer.com.

Made in the USA
Charleston, SC
18 May 2012